AF394496

The Mindful Mum

365 Peaceful Reflections and Daily Gratitude

Meg Sylvester

Contents

Welcome to Your Favourite Self

I wrote this book mum to mum. Not as someone who has it all figured out, but as someone who has been in it—who has felt exhausted by the weight of expectations, who has tried to win the imaginary award for personal development, who has spiraled in and out of "fixing" herself, only to realize she was never broken to begin with.

I spent years trying to get life right. I read the books, did the meditations, journaled my inner child into exhaustion, and chased every possible path to clarity and healing. But instead of feeling free, I felt tangled. Trapped in the pursuit of being my "best self," like peace was something I had to earn through sheer effort.

And while all that was happening, life was *lifeing*. I lost a parent. I was diagnosed with a chronic illness. I almost lost my marriage. I could have disappeared into that season. I almost did. But instead, I found my way back— not through discipline or more self-improvement, but through remembering who I already was. Through play. Through pleasure. Through joy. I felt alive again. I *feel* alive again. And I want that for you, too.

This is not a book about how to be a better mum. It's not about how to be a "better" version of yourself.

This is a book about you. A wild, vibrant, multi-layered soul who *also* happens to be a mum. Motherhood may be part of your story, but it is not *all* of your story. You don't need another self-help manual with a list of things you *should* be doing. You don't need more pressure to get it right.

What you need—what we all need—is a *reclamation*.

It's time to reclaim yourself, your joy, your light. It's time to remember what it feels like to wake up excited for your own life. To play again. To take yourself less seriously and take joy more seriously. This isn't about toxic positivity. I won't tell you to "just be happy" or pretend life isn't messy. Because it is. Some seasons are heavy. Some days, you'll struggle. That's not a sign that things are broken—it's a sign that you're living a real, full, complex human life.

But what if, even in those hard seasons, you had a way back to yourself? What if there was a way to return to yourself . . . not as a task but as a lifeline? A gentle, daily nudge toward joy, peace, satisfaction, and the electric fullness of being alive. That's what this book about: it's not meant not to "fix" you, but to bring you back to the magic that's been yours all along.

You've probably heard phrases like your "highest self" or your "best self." And while those ideas can be inspiring, they can also create pressure and yet another standard to meet, another version of yourself to become, another endless staircase to climb. I don't want you to strive for your best self. I want you to reconnect with your Favourite Self.

She's not some future version of you waiting on the other side of productivity, discipline, or checking off all the right boxes. She's already here. She's you, underneath the pressure, underneath the roles you've taken on, underneath the expectations that have weighed you down.

Your Favourite Self is the version of you that feels most alive.

She's playful, creative, bold, magnetic. She laughs more. She moves through life with curiosity and joy—not because everything is perfect, but because she trusts the flow of life and her own ability to create something meaningful within it. This book is about waking her up.

Most of us don't just wake up one day and forget who we are. It happens slowly, over time. We become caretakers first, people second. We internalize messaging that our worth is tied to productivity—that we have to earn rest, joy, or celebration. We start believing that our desires are optional, indulgent, or selfish. And slowly, we stop checking in with ourselves. We lose the small rituals that make us feel alive. We let guilt creep in when we do something just for us. And we wonder why life feels flat. The good news? Your Favourite Self has never left. She's just waiting for you to remember her.

You don't need permission to start. You don't need a perfect plan. You just need a little curiosity. A little space. A little *yes* to yourself.

Turn the page, and let's wake up the wild in you.

How to Use This Book

This book is a guide—a conversation between you and your Favourite Self. Each day builds on the last, gently stacking one small shift at a time. This book is meant to be read in order, because growth happens in layers. But what if you miss a day?

That's okay. This book isn't going anywhere. It will be right here, waiting for you with open arms.

Each day, you'll find:

- A quick insight to shift your perspective.
- A small action step—whether it's a mindset shift, a playful challenge, or a moment of reflection.

The book is divided into four phases, each with six categories that build on one another, guiding you toward your Favourite Self. **Phase One** helps you reconnect to your spark—where it flickers, what fuels it, and how to tend to it gently. **Phase Two** invites exploration. You'll play, get curious, try new things, and loosen the grip on perfection—creating for joy, not productivity. **Phase Three** builds confidence and helps shake limiting beliefs. **Phase Four** is about embodying your Favourite Self—the bold, joyous, authentic you.

This journey follows the **RISE framework**, a process I developed after years of supporting thousands of women through transformation. RISE offers small, intentional steps that build on each other—no dramatic overhauls, no pressure to leap before you're ready. Whether you're just waking up to what you want or starting to embody it more fully, this process meets you where you are and walks with you from there.

Each category explores a real, relevant, and personal topic. You'll move through a category every two weeks and within each, you'll go through the full RISE cycle, plus two built-in reflection days—one midway, one at the end—to pause, take inventory, and celebrate your growth. Here is what the RISE framework is designed to help you do:

1. **Recognize Days:** Noticing patterns, feelings, or sparks.
2. **Investigate:** Exploring ideas and asking playful or reflective questions.
3. **Shift:** Taking small actions or experimenting with new perspectives.
4. **Embody:** Integrating insights and celebrating progress.

Note: Phases Two and Four include extra days in the final category, offering more space to go deeper, integrate what you've discovered, and settle into the growth you've created.

I've made this manageable on purpose. From one mum to another—I get it. Some days you might be all in, feeling inspired and knocking out every action. Other days, you might barely skim a page while hiding in the bathroom from your kids.

Both are valid. It all counts.

You don't have to start on January 1. You can start any day, because every day is an opportunity. This book starts on Day 1, whenever that day falls for you. There is no "behind." There is only showing up when you can, how you can. Progress, not perfection.

Your only job? To keep coming back to yourself.

A Quick Note

Motherhood and personal growth do not have to be separate things.

Your kids will notice you dancing in the kitchen. They'll see you prioritizing your own joy. And when they do? They'll learn that it's safe to do the same for themselves. Transformation doesn't wait for perfect conditions—it lives in the real, messy, everyday moments.

That doesn't mean you have to include your kids in everything. It doesn't mean you don't get boundaries. Some things—your rituals, your journaling, your solo walks—get to be just for you. Some days, they'll be part of it: sitting beside you as you breathe, watching you light a candle, or asking questions during your meditation. It doesn't have to be perfect, just real. That softening of boundaries? That's part of the experience too. Make this journey possible, not impossible. Even five minutes of connection with your Favourite Self is powerful.

Lastly, some prompts may touch on tender topics like guilt, shame, or your relationship with self-care, such as food and movement. If something stirs deeper emotions, you don't have to navigate it alone—consider reaching out to a therapist, counselor, coach, or medical professional. This book is here to help you reclaim your spark, which means touching on some hard stuff, but it's not a substitute for professional care. And remember: you never have to engage with any prompt that feels uncomfortable or overwhelming. Skip, pause, or return later—your well-being comes first, always.

Phase One: Wake the Wild

Before you can feel fully alive again, you have to notice where you've been on autopilot.

Phase One (Days 1 to 84) is about waking up—not with a jolt, but with steady attention. You'll slow down enough to hear yourself again and begin to notice the small sparks you've been brushing past. This is where you start to meet her—your Favourite Self.

On Days 1 to 14, you'll keep it simple: small shifts, small pauses, sustainable choices, and a softer relationship with yourself. You'll start to build trust and meet your Favourite Self in real time.

As the days unfold, between Days 15 to 28, you'll begin to track what feels good, notice what drains you, and start making room for more of what helps you feel like yourself.

Next, throughout Days 29 to 42, you'll explore nourishment as a deeper form of self-care—one that goes beyond food and movement to include rest, joy, boundaries, and emotional presence. This is about shifting from pressure and performance to inner kindness and connection, so you can support yourself in ways that feel intuitive, grounding, and true.

As your spark grows, so does your courage. In Days 43 to 56, you'll practice loosening the grip of old conditioning and letting instinct have more say.

Then curiosity steps in. Between Days 57 to 70, you'll follow nudges, play with possibility, and start to reframe old beliefs. Instead of pressure, you'll meet yourself with openness and wonder.

You'll close out this phase with Days 71 to 84. You'll be guided toward embodying your Favourite Self. You'll name her, call her forward, and practice showing up as her in your everyday life. One small step at a time.

Day 1
Mindful Moments

This is the start of creating a more fulfilling life by building trust with yourself through small, meaningful actions. Lasting change happens through tuning in and tending to yourself in ways that feel doable. This is where you begin to feel into your Favourite Self—not as some perfect version far off in the distance, but as the spark that's been pulsing within you all along— however subtle it may now seem. You'll offer her a soft hello. You'll extend your hand. Little by little, you will begin to move together. Start where you are, with what you have. Small is powerful. Small is enough. And small, repeated with care, creates real momentum.

How often as a parent do you ignore your needs, minimize your exhaustion, or brush off your own comfort like it's a luxury instead of a necessity?

Me Moment: *Check in with yourself and ask, What do I need right now?*

- *If the answer is rest, take five minutes to close your eyes or simply breathe.*

- *If it's nourishment, eat something that makes you feel good—not just fueled, but cared for.*

- *If it's comfort, wrap yourself in a blanket, hold your own hand, or listen to a song that soothes you.*

- *Every time you notice a need today, pause and remind yourself: I am worth tending to.*

Day 2: Notice Yourself

When was the last time you actually *noticed* yourself? Not how well you're keeping up with everything and everyone. Just you. It's easy to slip into autopilot throughout the day—meeting responsibilities, handling tasks—without pausing to acknowledge that you are a whole person, outside of what you do for others. Today, take a moment to acknowledge your whole, multifaceted self—the person you are beyond your roles, your tasks, your to-do list.

Me Moment: *Stand in front of a mirror, hands on your heart, and look yourself in the eyes. Say out loud: "I see you. You matter." Let this be a homecoming to yourself—a small, sacred moment of seeing, and being seen.*

Day 3: That's Enough, Janet!

If your best friend talked to you the way you talk to yourself, would you still be friends? Most of us have an inner voice that is harsh and unforgiving, reinforcing self-doubt. But that voice is not you. It's a learned script shaped by past experiences and fears.

Me Moment: *Today, name your inner critic—like "Janet" or "Ms. Perfect"—to separate it from the truth. When it says, "You're not enough," reply, "Not today, Janet." If it persists, remind her gently, "I know you're trying to protect me, but I'm choosing a new way now." Each time you respond with grounded authority, you're laying the foundation for a more peaceful and satisfying life.*

Day 4: Your Favourite Self

Today, you're meeting the version of you who is free, joyful, and fully alive—the part of you who already knows who she is and moves through life without apology, hesitation, or guilt. She already exists inside of you and is ready to be called forward now.

Me Moment: *Find a quiet space, close your eyes, and breathe deeply. Imagine a version of you who feels free, steady, alive, and connected to her spark. Notice how she carries herself, how she feels in your body—not out there, but already within you. You don't have to force it, just sense where that energy might live: in your chest, your gut, your hands. Wherever she stirs, give her a home. Trust that she's part of you—not a fantasy, not a goal, but a truth already in motion. Throughout this journey, you'll keep calling her forward until she no longer feels separate at all.*

Day 5: It Starts with Ease

Joy isn't something that happens to you—it's a state of mind you cultivate. It's the ability to witness, receive, and meet life with openness and delight. And it begins with ease. Ease is the soil where joy blooms. It's the softening, the loosening of the grip, the breath before the laugh. When you practice creating ease, you expand your capacity to experience joy again and again. Creating ease in your life can look like asking: *How can I let this be easier? Where can I soften my approach, even slightly?*

Me Moment: *Today, practice noticing where you can catch or create ease. When you feel tension rising, whether in your shoulders, your schedule, or your thinking, pause and ask, How can I let this be easier? If you find yourself gripping—mentally or physically—loosen your hold. Ease is always available.*

Day 6: Gratitude, But Make It Sticky

Gratitude is a powerful force, but in order to activate its magnetism, you have to *feel* it. Creating generic lists of things to feel gratitude for, like "health, family, job," can fall flat because they don't activate your senses or emotions. The secret? *Specificity.* When you zoom in on the tiny, vivid details, gratitude becomes real, alive, and magnetic—it sticks.

Me Moment: *Write a ridiculously specific gratitude list. Instead of, I'm grateful for my children, try, I'm grateful for the way my kiddo waved at me from across the playground. Specificity helps you tune into the richness that's already around you. Your brain starts collecting even more good things, training itself to see the good stuff instead of just waiting for it to appear.*

Day 7: Look How Far You've Come

Congrats! You made it through your first six days. That's six days of showing up for yourself, six days of noticing, questioning, and beginning to shift. Change happens in small actions stacked on top of each other. This is progress, not perfection. You're doing it.

Me Moment: *Ask yourself, What's shifted in the past week? What's one moment where I felt more like me? What's something I'm curious to explore next? Write your answers down or just sit with them for a moment. You don't have to have it all figured out. You just have to keep showing up.*

Day 8: Permission to Pause

Many of us default to saying yes without even realizing it. *Sure, no problem* slips out before we've checked in with ourselves. But a yes given too quickly can cost you time and attention you'd rather spend elsewhere. Pausing is powerful—it creates space to ask: *Do I actually want this?*

Me Moment: *Practice buying time today. When someone asks for something, try this phrase: Let me get back to you. Notice how it feels to insert a pause before you commit. What opens up when you give yourself that space?*

Day 9: New Evidence

The ego, your mind's protective narrator, loves to be right. It doesn't care if the story is helpful or harmful. If it believes *life is hard,* it will scan your reality for evidence. If it thinks *I'm never chosen,* it will find proof. Not because it wants you to suffer, but because it craves certainty more than truth. Lasting change starts with your willingness to interrupt that. You can notice the story and decide not to let it run the show.

Me Moment: *Choose one pervasive thought that's been looping in your mind lately. Something like, "Nothing ever works out for me," or "I'm too scattered." Write it down. Say it out loud. Then create a comeback statement. Something grounded but firm, like, "Actually, I've made a lot of things work or I'm learning to see my variety as strength, not a flaw." This is how new pathways start to form.*

Day 10: So Turned On

To be turned on is to be awake to your life: more present, more connected. You begin to notice the deeper world around you—how it's humming with life, how it makes you feel. It's like raising an antenna that's been pushed down. You start to tune in instead of moving through the motions.

Me Moment: *Reflect on the phrase "turned on to life." What does it mean to you? Where have you felt turned off or disconnected lately? What's one small way you could turn the dial up today through sensation, attention, or presence?*

Day 11: No More Shrinking

You know that reflex—the one where you soften your voice, add a little "just" to your sentences, or apologize for things that don't require an apology? The one where you explain why you're doing something before anyone even asks? That's shrinking. It's the automatic instinct to make yourself smaller, more digestible, easier to take in. But today, you're flipping the script.

Me Moment: *For the next twenty-four hours, pay attention to moments when you shrink yourself. Each time you catch it, pause and change the narrative. Instead of saying, "Sorry I'm rambling," try, "I love talking about this." Stand in what you are saying with confidence.*

Day 12: Me First

Most of us start the day by absorbing—emails, texts, social media, news. Before we've had a thought of our own, we're already filled up with external noise. When you begin your morning tuned in to others, it becomes harder to hear yourself. Shifting this pattern—by tuning into your own energy first—can help you anchor into your own needs before the world starts making demands.

Me Moment: *Before your feet hit the floor, take one quiet moment for yourself. Place your hand over your heart. Breathe deeply. Say a gentle hello to yourself.*

Day 13: Your True Yes

Not every urge is worth following. Some are distractions, numbing, or self-sabotage. The ones to pay attention to are the small, genuine desires that energize you and bring joy or peace. Saying yes to aligned desires—even tiny ones—builds trust with yourself.

Me Moment: *When a desire pops up today, pause and ask: Will this leave me feeling more alive, lighter, or more connected—or drained, guilty, or checked-out? Use that gut check as your compass.*

Day 14: Reflect and Celebrate

You made it through the first two weeks. That might not seem like a big deal, but it is. Showing up for yourself, even in small, imperfect ways, builds real, sustainable change.

Me Moment: *Acknowledge what's shifted. Ask: What's one small thing I've done differently since Day 1? What made me feel more me? There is no "right" answer. Just keep showing up, one page at a time.*

Day 15

The Spark Within

Now that you've started to come home to yourself, it's time to tune in to what's really happening beneath the surface—what's fueling you and what's quietly wearing you down.

This is a gentle exploration of your life-force energy and becoming more aware of how your body, mood, and spirit respond to different people, places, habits, and expectations. When you begin to pay attention to what lights you up—and what leaves you depleted—you naturally start to choose differently, more consciously.

Most of us have been conditioned to focus on what's wrong—what's missing, what needs fixing—so that we can make it better. But today, we will start shifting the gaze of the mind's eye to notice what's already working. Track the moments when life feels good, even in the smallest ways. Not everything needs to be life-changing to be worth noticing. The more you acknowledge what feels good, the more you invite it in. This is a powerful calibration that when done enough, can shift your entire reality over time.

Me Moment: *For the next twenty-four hours, track only the good. Write down or mentally note each small moment of ease or delight. Notice how your body feels in those moments. This is about practicing presence with what lights you up.*

Day 16: Energy Audit

Interactions, habits, and environments all carry a certain weight. Some leave you feeling nourished, some leave you drained, and some are simply neutral. Paying closer attention reveals patterns you may have overlooked. An audit helps you see where your energy naturally rises and where it quietly slips away, so you can make choices that support your spark.

Me Moment: *Keep three running columns today: fuels me, drains me, neutral. Add to them as you move through your day. At the end, review your lists and choose one small adjustment—something that invites more of what fuels you or releases a drain.*

Day 17: Expand

Sometimes, a catalyst for your own expansion comes from seeing someone else live a life you didn't yet know was available to you. Expanders show us what's available by cracking open the window of possibility. They're not idols or blueprints but proof that more is possible. Maybe it's a confident friend, an inspiring public figure, or someone in your community who makes you think, *If they can do it, maybe I can too.*

Me Moment: *Think of someone who expands your sense of possibility. What is it about them that stirs something in you—their confidence, creativity, or presence? Notice the feelings that rise when you imagine stepping into that space for yourself. What does their example suggest you're ready to explore in your own life?*

Day 18: Blame Game Redefined

When life feels frustrating, it's tempting to reach for blame. The kids, your partner, your boss, the traffic—someone must be at fault for why you feel stuck, overwhelmed, or behind. But blame doesn't move us forward. It just keeps us swirling in frustration. The truth is: blame is a signal that you feel powerless. Instead of spiraling outward, reach inward. Beneath the irritation is usually a longing—for rest, for acknowledgement, for more ease, or something else. When you can name what you actually want, you free yourself from circling around the problem and can move toward solution that feels supportive.

Me Moment: *Notice one moment today when blame shows up, whether it's loud or subtle. Pause, breathe, and ask yourself: What's the deeper need underneath this blame? Is it rest? A boundary? A sense of control? A longing to feel seen? Get honest and write it down. This is how you start to shift—not by fixing everything, but by meeting yourself in the truth.*

Day 19: Seal the Leaks

Drains on your well-being don't just come from obvious stressors—they sneak in the background through things left unfinished. The email you keep postponing. The closet you keep meaning to organise. The "yes" you didn't mean but now carry. These leaks may seem small, but together they pull on your reserves.

Me Moment: *Today, identify one energy leak you've been tolerating. It could be a nagging thought, an undone task, or a boundary you've ignored. Take one concrete step to close it—send the text, cancel the plan, finish the thing. Notice how much lighter you feel when you reclaim that lost capacity.*

Day 20: Stop "Shoulding" Yourself

The voice of "should" is sneaky. It tells you to wake up earlier, work harder, do more—not as a choice, but as a requirement. It dresses itself up as discipline or responsibility, but underneath, it's just pressure you've picked up. True motivation, on the other hand, comes from within. It creates space for connection, fulfilment, and ease.

Me Moment: *As you go through your day, catch the voice of "should" in real time. Pause and ask: Is this my true motivation, or just an expectation I've absorbed? Try reframing I should _________ into I choose to _________. Notice how the shift feels.*

Day 21: Tiny Shifts, Big Magic

Let's pause and reflect. Take a moment to look back at your notes from the past few days. Do any patterns emerge? Are certain activities, people, or environments consistently supporting or draining your energy? Tiny shifts, done consistently, change everything.

Me Moment: *Write down three things that reliably make you feel good, then write down one small shift you can make to invite more of that into your life.*

Day 22: Redefining Clarity

We've been conditioned to think clarity is a set of answers—answers to questions like *Who am I? What's my purpose?* But what if clarity isn't an answer at all? What if it's a state of mind—a spaciousness, a stillness beneath the noise and expectations? It's the inner environment that allows truth to rise. When you're connected to that kind of clarity, there's less urgency to force, prove, or explain. Your full expression flows more naturally.

Me Moment: *Set a timer for five minutes and simply focus on connecting to your place of inner knowing. No forcing, no analysing. Just tune in to your breath. Familiarize yourself with that feeling. Maybe it feels like a still lake, or a clear sky. That's clarity, and it's always available.*

Day 23: Let it Go

Growth isn't just measured by what you achieve—it's often revealed by what you let go of: the moment you didn't spiral, the comment you didn't take personally, the worry you didn't let take root. Every time you choose peace over proving or grace over spiraling, that's a win worth celebrating.

Me Moment: *When you catch yourself gripping—trying to explain, prove, control, or overanalyse—pause. Take a breath. Choose the lighter path. Even if it's just in your mind, say, I don't need to hold on to this. Then move on. One small release at a time, you're building something softer, stronger, and freer.*

Day 24: Already Abundant

An abundant life begins in the present. In the way you notice what's already good. In how you experience pleasure, presence, and the soft richness woven into your everyday. The more you give reverence to what's already here, the more you train your mind and body to recognize abundance, not as a future reward, but as a feeling available now. You begin to invite more in by honouring what you already have.

Me Moment: *Open your fridge, your closet, or your calendar and look for proof of enough. Instead of focusing on what's missing, name what's already here to support you. This is how you remind yourself that abundance isn't waiting somewhere ahead—it's all around you.*

Day 25: Reverse the Formula

Think about the people who light up a room when they walk in. It's not because the room was already joyful, it's because they're plugged in to their own light. They carry the vibe they want to experience, and the world rises to meet it. Choose to bring life to the moment, instead of waiting for the moment to bring life to you.

Me Moment: *Today, lead with joy, ease, or confidence by tending to your energy first. Slow and soften to invite in more ease. Move with confidence before you feel certain. Drop into gratitude before the thing happens. Say thank you out loud—for anything—and notice how your reality catches up.*

Day 26: Hype Track

Music is energy. It stirs emotion, impacts your mood, and calls forward parts of you that are pulsing beneath the surface. Every story has a soundtrack, and a playlist can be a portal back to your essence.

Me Moment: *Take time to intentionally create a playlist that carries the spirit of your Favourite Self—bold, soulful, playful, etc. Play it when you're getting ready, on your way to work, or when you need a pick-me-up.*

Day 27: Proof Points

Most of the time, we brush past small, everyday moments without thinking much about them. But those moments can be proof that life is helping you out. A parking spot opening right when you pull in could mean things are lining up for you. A friend texting just when you needed a lift could be a reminder that you're not alone. When you choose to see these neutral moments as support, you train yourself to notice that good things are already happening.

Me Moment: *Look back at the last forty-eight hours. Pick one or two neutral moments—something you might normally ignore. Now, spin them into proof that life is conspiring in your favour.*

Day 28: A Month into Joy

What you notice is what you attract. Take a moment to reflect on your previous days. What have you learned about what makes you feel alive?

Me Moment: *Write down your reflections as a powerful way to seal in the positive momentum you're creating. What themes, feelings, or patterns have you noticed over the past few weeks? What brings you ease, lightness, or a spark of energy?*

Day 29

Nourishment as Care

Caring for yourself is a way to nourish your dreams, fuel your life-force, and create a life that feels aligned from the inside out. The way you nourish yourself impacts everything—from clarity to confidence, joy, and your ability to show up for what matters most.

In this section, we'll explore self-care through a fresh lens—not as obligations or boxes to check, but as everyday invitations to support yourself. That might look like savouring food that fuels you, moving your body in ways that feel good, taking a deep breath, leaning into pleasure, making space for play, or simply being present. You'll reflect on what's working, release what's not, and create perspectives that align with how you want to feel. Nourishment is a gift. You deserve to receive it.

The way you approach self-care has likely been shaped by many influences—family, culture, media, and silent expectations. For many of us, these influences have morphed the concept of self-care into pressure: to perform, to prove, to push through. Today is about gently checking in with where you are, without judgement or agenda.

Me Moment: *Take a quiet moment to reflect on your relationship with self-care. Does caring for yourself feel like nourishment or obligation? Pleasure or pressure? What beliefs or emotions have shaped that relationship? How would you like it to feel moving forward—gentle, joyful, intuitive, free? There's no right answer. Just write freely and see what surfaces.*

Day 30: Devotion in Motion

Moving your body in ways that feel nourishing is a practical form of self-devotion. When movement is fueled by pressure to look a certain way, it feels like obligation. But when it's rooted in your desire to feel good, it becomes a way of honouring yourself—body, mind, and spirit.

Me Moment: *How can movement support you physically, emotionally, mentally, and spiritually? Reflect on how pleasurable movement can serve as a form of devotion to the life you are creating. Then write your personal why. For example: I move because I feel good, and I deserve to feel good.*

Day 31: Micro Moves

Building a new rhythm with movement takes time, intention, and attention. For busy moms, carving time to work out may not always feel realistic. Building a rhythm of self-care doesn't require big gestures. Small, consistent choices create momentum, helping you reconnect with your body in ways that feel supportive and doable.

Me Moment: *Swap one everyday moment for a burst of self-care. That might be gentle movement like a five-minute walk, stretching before bed, or stepping outside for fresh air. It could also be saying no to something draining. Try it just because it feels good. At the end of the day, check in: How did it feel?*

Day 32: Make it Real

The best goals are sticky. They're doable, measurable, and rooted in something that matters to you. Think of the life you're building. What kind of movement would support it? Maybe you're building strength to play with your kids, mirroring your inner resilience, or releasing stagnancy to feel more creative and clearer.

Me Moment: *Name one way movement could support you this week—something that feels doable and gentle. Then ask: What does this intention represent for me? Confidence? Vitality? Ease?*

Day 33: Embodied Play

Self-care through movement doesn't always have to be a serious production. It can be lighthearted, silly, and energizing. Reclaiming joy in how you move invites you to connect with your body in a new way. What used to delight you? What could feel good now?

Me Moment: *Make a list of playful ways you like to recharge. Make up a dance, roller skate, hula hoop, go for a jog peppered with dance breaks, do a sensual stretch in the sun. Then choose one to try today. Think of this as a moment of delight. Nothing to track. Nothing to earn. Just joy.*

NOURISH

Day 34: Generate Momentum

When you move in ways that feel good to your body, you create space for clarity and focus. You don't have to wait for motivation—you can nurture it by engaging in movement modalities that support your mental health and strengthen your sense of possibility in daily life.

Me Moment: *Today, explore how moving in ways that feel good to you impacts your mental well-being and sense of motivation. Engage in a form of movement that you love—maybe it's dancing with your kids, gardening, or stretching—and simply notice how it influences your mood, focus, and outlook. As you're moving, imagine connecting to the wellspring of vitality that lives within you. Let it nourish your spirit.*

Day 35: Keep it Up

You've spent this week reconnecting with self-care as a form of nourishment. Perhaps you've released pressure or learned to move in new ways that feel good. You've set the foundation. The next step is building momentum and staying in it.

Me Moment: *What parts of this week felt most supportive? Why does continuing a self-care practice matter to you? Write down one way you'll continue your momentum moving forward. This could be a weekly goal, an inspiring practice, or a reminder of why it matters. Keep it simple.*

Day 36: Rewrite the Rules

Culture, family, and media all shape how we view self-care. Maybe you grew up seeing parents who never rested or learned that women should put everyone else first. Maybe media taught you self-care is something you buy. Today is your chance to notice those old messages.

Me Moment: *List a few beliefs you've absorbed about caring for yourself—physically, emotionally, mentally, or spiritually. Which ones still influence you? Which are you ready to rewrite?*

Day 37: Rewrite the Rules

Culture, family, and media all shape how we view self-care. Maybe you grew up seeing parents who never rested or learned that women should put everyone else first. Maybe media taught you self-care is something you buy. Today is your chance to notice those old messages.

Me Moment: *List a few beliefs you've absorbed about caring for yourself—physically, emotionally, mentally, or spiritually. Which ones still influence you? Which are you ready to rewrite?*

Day 38: Breath as Nourishment

Breath is one of the simplest and most reliable ways to nourish yourself. A deep inhale can energize, a slow exhale can calm, and steady attention can bring you back to the present. Every breath is an opportunity to restore balance—no effort, no equipment, just you.

Me Moment: *Pause for three slow, intentional breaths. Notice how your body responds—do you feel steadier, softer, more awake? Today, in moments of stress, distraction, or fatigue, try calling on your breath as a tool for nourishment.*

Day 39: Mindful Nourishment

When you're rushed, distracted, or stuck in old patterns, you may lose sight of the fact that taking care of yourself is an act of self-respect. Things like food can turn into an afterthought, a battleground, or a source of support. Every meal is an opportunity to care for both your current and your future self. Today is about noticing the intention behind how you feed yourself, and asking whether it reflects the care you truly deserve.

Me Moment: *Choose one meal or snack today and approach it as an act of love. Slow down. Choose what feels supportive. Nourish yourself like someone worth caring for, because you are.*

Day 40: Fuel Your Flow

Many moms move through the day on autopilot, skipping meals or grabbing whatever's nearby. But nourishment isn't just food, it's a reminder that you matter. A snack, a deep breath, or a quiet moment alone—fueling yourself is an act of self-care, not indulgence.

Me Moment: *Today, take a moment to check in with yourself before a snack or meal. Ask gently: What would feel supportive right now? Maybe it's food, rest, or a moment to breathe. Whatever it is, honour it.*

Day 41: Indulge Yourself

Food isn't just fuel. It's colour, texture, pleasure, and life. It connects us to memory, culture, creativity, and celebration. Nourishing yourself well is a reminder that you're worth the pleasure of a good meal. Many women have been taught that indulgence is something to feel guilty about. But pleasure is part of living well, and food can absolutely be one of the ways you access it.

Me Moment: *What foods light you up—by flavor, texture, or memory? Eat something that delights you today. Notice how it feels to let food be a source of delight.*

Day 42: Creating Sustenance

How you care for yourself shapes your energy, clarity, mood, and sense of self. When you bring presence to nourishment, everything aligns. You've taken steps toward a more supportive relationship with yourself—now keep that connection going.

Me Moment: *What shifted this week in your self-care? What felt supportive or freeing? What do you want to carry forward? Name one small practice to stay connected to that energy.*

Day 43

Wild Child

The word *wild*, in its true form, does not mean *reckless*. Real wildness, the kind that feels good in your bones, is simply the part of you that refuses to live on mute.

Your wildness is your original rhythm—the part of you that existed before the rules, roles, and expectations took hold. It's instinctive. Untamed. A deep inner knowing that says, *There's more life to live here*, even when everything around you says to settle.

Over time, layers of conditioning—societal, cultural, generational—begin to press down. You learn to tone it down, smooth your edges, and prioritize being acceptable over being true. Sometimes, *you* even become your own cage—holding back the parts of you that feel too loud, too emotional, too tender, too wild. The parts that once felt free can start to feel shameful, or even dangerous.

This is an invitation to loosen the grip of what you've been taught to suppress so that you can begin to reconnect to reclaim your voice. Think of a wildflower—growing on its own terms, messy and magnificent, full of thorns, blooms, and buzzing life. Your wildness is meant to be felt, expressed, inhabited. It holds texture, depth, unpredictability. That's what makes it beautiful.

Me Moment: *Today, ask yourself, What does wild feel like for me? Not the version shaped to impress, but the one that pulses with something real. Write down three small ways that energy wants to move through you. Then imagine what it would look like to let it. There's no right answer. Just write freely and see what surfaces.*

Day 44: Break the Rules

There are the rules we have to follow, and then there are the invisible ones we just think we have to. The ones that whisper, "Good girls don't do that," or, "You're too old for this." Rules that shrink us without us even noticing.

Me Moment: *Today, reflect on one unspoken rule you've been following without questioning. Maybe it's about how you "should" dress, speak, rest, or create. Name it. Then ask yourself, What would it feel like to gently break that rule?*

Day 45: What Judgement Really Means

Sometimes the parts of others we judge most—the bold, the loud, the carefree—are mirrors showing us our wild parts that we've tucked away. It's not really about them. It's about the part of you that's longing to take up more space, to be seen, to be free. Get curious about your judgments. What is your spirit yearning to reclaim?

Me Moment: *Think back to a recent moment when you judged another woman—maybe for being too loud, too confident, too something. What might she have been expressing that you secretly long to free within yourself? Write it down. You already carry that wildness too.*

Day 46: Did You Clip Your Wings?

At some point, you might've started taming yourself without even realizing it. Maybe you turned the volume down on your boldness. Maybe you learned to smile instead of speak up. Maybe you started trading wonder for what's practical. Today, you get to ask, *Where did I clip my own wings? And where might I be ready to let them grow back?*

Me Moment: *Take the time to answer the following question: Is there a characteristic from your younger years that you "clipped" in order to make yourself smaller, quieter, or more acceptable?*

Day 47: Calling or Conditioning?

Sometimes what we think we want isn't what we really want, it's a story we've absorbed from families, schools, culture, or even well-meaning mentors. We're handed rules about what a "good life" looks like, what success means, who we're supposed to be and more. Over time, those stories can drown out the voice of your own true desire. Learning to recognize what's truly yours versus what's been handed to you helps you make choices that feel aligned with your true self, not just what's expected.

Me Moment: *Pick one thing you've been chasing, wanting, or feeling pulled toward lately. Ask yourself, Is this a true yearning from my soul or something I learned I was "supposed" to want? If it's something you're "supposed" to want, how freeing would it feel to let it go?*

Day 48: The Truth About Guilt

Real guilt is a physiological response. It shows up after a behaviour that violates our internal sense of right and wrong—something that helps us grow, take accountability, and move forward differently. But conditioned guilt? That's something else entirely. Conditioned guilt is learned and modeled. It's a silent set of rules we've been taught to follow, especially as women and mothers. We feel guilty not because we've done something wrong, but because we've been told we're *supposed* to feel guilty. Spend time alone? Guilt. Set a boundary? Guilt. Feel joy outside your role as a caregiver? Guilt.

Me Moment: *Today, examine your relationship with guilt. What's something you've felt guilty for lately? Ask yourself, Was this real guilt—something that violated my values? Or was this conditioned guilt—something I've absorbed from society? If it's the latter, give yourself permission to release it. You were never meant to carry that weight.*

Day 49: Tiny Leaps

You've spent the past few days getting closer to your real self—the part of you that's a little less edited, a little more electric. You've noticed old rules, old masks, and old stories that you don't have to carry anymore. Today, honour that growth.

Me Moment: *What have you noticed about your wildness? Where have you softened, opened, or reclaimed a part of yourself? And what tiny leap forward are you feeling curious (or brave enough) to take next?*

Day 50: The Wlld Within

You are not separate from nature—you *are* nature. The same intelligence that moves tides, blooms flowers, and stirs the wind lives in you, too. When you feel disconnected, boxed in, or unsure of yourself, reconnecting to the natural world can remind you of your own rhythm, your own truth.

Me Moment: *The elements—earth, water, fire, air—aren't just outside you; they are you. Grounded. Fluid. Fierce. Free. Each one mirrors a part of your essence. Which element feels most like you right now? What qualities of that element live in you? Instead of resisting your inherent nature, how can you honour it? Are you craving more grounding, more movement, more boldness, or more ease? What would it look like to honour that part of yourself today?*

Day 51: Reclaiming "No"

Protecting your wildness doesn't always mean chasing new adventures. Sometimes it means guarding your energy like sacred ground. Every unnecessary "yes" puts another fence around your freedom. Reclaiming your "no" is how you keep the gate open for what truly matters.

Me Moment: *Identify one request, habit, or expectation you're ready to decline. Say "no"—gently, firmly, without apology. Notice how it feels in your body to take that stand. Does it feel like release? Relief? Strength?*

Day 52: No Disclaimers

Many of us weaken our own voices before they've even had a chance to be heard. We tack on disclaimers like, *This might sound silly . . .* or *It's not that good but . . .*, to soften the blow of potential judgement. But those qualifiers don't protect you, they dilute you. They tell the world (and yourself) your ideas aren't as worthy as they truly are. It's time to see what happens when you stop cushioning and start standing behind your gifts, talents, and strengths.

Me Moment: *Today, share something—an opinion, an idea, a creation, even your outfit—without qualifiers. No self-deprecation, no apologies, no disclaimers. Let it stand on its own. Notice how it feels to give your expression its full weight.*

Day 53: Let It Be Easy

Overcomplicating things is a form of control. And control blocks flow, joy, and that spark of vitality. Society has conditioned many of us to believe that struggling, complexity and even suffering make an effort worthy. But the truth is, ease is not the enemy. Ease is a sign of trust and flow. You can't receive with a closed fist. Today, you're softening your grip.

Me Moment: *Choose one thing you normally overcomplicate— getting dressed, making dinner, writing an email—and just see if you can make it a tiny bit easier . . . a tiny bit softer. These everyday tasks can quietly turn into pressure: trying to find the perfect outfit, cook the ideal meal, or word things just right. Today, let it be simple.*

Day 54: Ugly Dance

Many of us have picked up the idea that the way we express ourselves needs to meet a standard: to be pretty, to be polished, to be correct. That there's a right way and a wrong way to create and move through the world. Today, you begin to untangle yourself from that story.

Me Moment: *Turn on a song that stirs something inside you. Close your eyes and invite the wild within to move you. Ask your body how it wants to move and indulge that feeling. Challenge yourself to be wild, messy, and even strange. This is about building trust with your body's wisdom, one unpolished, glorious step at a time.*

Day 55: Into the Wild

One of the most freeing realizations is that the fear of judgement you've built up in your head doesn't actually exist. People aren't watching or scrutinizing you nearly as much as your inner critic would have you believe. And if they are, it says more about them than it does about you. The less effort you spend worrying about what others think, the freer you—and your inner wild—become. That shift is pure liberation.

Me Moment: *Now you get to bring your wildness out into the world. Pick a low-stakes place—the grocery store, the gas station, the library—and wear something that feels like a nod to your inner wild child. Notice what happens, not out there, but in you. Remind yourself: I am free to be all-the-way me.*

Day 56: See the Blooms

You've spent the past two weeks tending to your inner wildness like a garden—giving it light, space, attention. Letting it unfurl in its own time. Like a wildflower, it grows when it's left to be unrestricted and untouched by expectation. Just allowed to exist.

Me Moment: *What's begun to blossom? What feels softer, wilder, freer? Take a moment to notice the places where your inner wildness has started to stretch toward the sun.*

Day 57

Soft Wonder

Curiosity is an innate superpower, one many of us have forgotten how to use. We've been taught to chase certainty, seek outcomes, and stay on track. But wonder works differently. It asks us to pause: to lean in, to follow the tug, even when we don't know where it's leading.

Think of curiosity like a muscle. The more you use it, the more naturally it moves. With practice, your world starts to feel more alive—full of glimmers, nudges, and unexpected invitations. You begin to notice beauty where you used to rush past it and possibility where you used to feel uncertain.

Curiosity is the gateway to wonder—and wonder opens the door to deeper levels of fulfilment and a more meaningful connection to life itself.

Most of us are so focused on being efficient, certain, or productive that we miss the quiet, magical nudges from within beckoning us to something deeper. The second glance at the pottery class flyer. The urge to Google something random. The tiny flicker that says, *Hey, look over here.* But that's not you, not anymore. You're now one of the ones who answers the call to explore, to wonder, to follow the gentle tug toward something new—not because you *have* to but because you *get* to.

Me Moment: *Catch one tiny spark of curiosity today. It might be a subject you suddenly want to learn about, a hobby that catches your eye, or even a new song that makes you feel something. No pressure to act on it—just notice it.*

Day 58: Practice Curiosity

We are wired to seek answers. Certainty feels safe. But when you rush to explain, define, or categorize every intuitive nudge, you close the door on possibility. You trade wonder for control, and in doing so, you shrink the space where something bigger could unfold. Today is about building a little more tolerance for mystery.

Me Moment: *Practice being open-minded. If you notice yourself rushing to a conclusion—about yourself, a situation, or someone else—pause and replace analysis with openness. Ask yourself, What else could be true here? Let the question hang in the air without forcing an answer.*

Day 59: Force or Effort?

Forcing something—whether it's a decision, a dream, or a version of yourself—often signals misalignment. It drains you, closes you off, keeps you gripping to things you may not want to. Effort, on the other hand, is different. Effort comes with momentum, movement, and purpose. It asks something of you, but it doesn't ask you to betray yourself. The key is learning to feel the difference.

Me Moment: *Where in your life do you feel like you're forcing— gritting your teeth, pushing upstream, overriding your instincts? And where do you feel a natural pull . . . toward a project, idea, or dream that's energizing, even if it requires effort? Reflect on how forcing something and being pulled toward something each feel different in your body. What might shift if you stopped forcing and started following what feels true?*

Day 60: Ready, Set, Reframe

The parts of yourself you've learned to label as "wrong" or "broken" may actually hold your greatest gifts. Sensitivity can mean attunement. Messiness can mean creativity. Restlessness can mean passion. Or feeling "all over the place" may mean you are multi-passionate. What you call a flaw might just be strength in disguise.

Me Moment: *Choose one trait you've tried to "fix." Instead of judging it, get curious. Explore how it could serve you. What's the hidden strength inside it? Write down a reframe that honours this part of you.*

Day 61: Origin Story

Every belief about yourself started somewhere. Maybe it came from a comment that stung, an expectation you absorbed, or a pattern you repeated until it felt like truth. But beliefs aren't facts—they're just old stories. You get to track them back and rewrite the narrative.

Me Moment: *Pick one belief you carry about yourself. Ask yourself: Where did this begin? Whose voice echoes in it? Then imagine retelling the story in your own voice—one rooted in compassion, not criticism.*

CURIOSITY

Day 62: Feel It to Free It

Beliefs don't just live in the mind; they imprint on the body: a clenched jaw, a pit in your stomach, a subtle tightness in your chest. These sensations are signals from your body, pointing to feelings or beliefs waiting to be noticed. When you bring awareness to them, the grip of old stories begins to loosen. Tension softens, and space opens for new understanding.

Me Moment: *Choose one belief that you've uncovered recently. Notice how it shows up in your body—maybe a heaviness, a flutter, or a knot. Place a hand there and breathe into it with warmth and curiosity. Imagine that spot softening, like opening a window in a room that's been closed for too long. Your awareness is enough to begin a shift.*

Day 63: Curiosity Cracked It Open

Look how far you've come in just a few days of asking questions instead of demanding answers. Curiosity cracked something open. It made space for new possibilities, perhaps even a new version of you. It loosened old patterns and invited you to witness yourself with fresh eyes.

Me Moment: *In the past week, where did curiosity awaken something inside you? What new truth about yourself feels a little more available, a little more real?*

Day 64: Choose a New "What If"

Your mind is powerful, and it's been rehearsing old "what if" fears for a long time. *What if I fail? What if I look ridiculous?* But what if today, you chose a different "what if"? *What if it works? What if you thrive? What if it's even better than you imagined?* Small shifts like these open entirely new pathways, helping you to imagine—and ultimately create—a more vibrant life for yourself.

Me Moment: *Today, if you catch yourself in a negative "what if" spiral, flip it. Choose a hopeful, mischievous, or slightly outrageous new "what if" to follow instead.*

Day 65: Habit or Free Will?

You make a habit, and then the habit makes you. Over time, many of your daily actions stop being conscious choices. They become patterns, wired into your brain for efficiency. Some habits are supportive (like brushing your teeth every morning). Others are just old programming that no longer fits who you're becoming (like checking your phone first thing every morning before taking a moment to yourself). Today is about getting curious: *Am I choosing this, or just repeating it?* You're not here to burn it all down. You're here to notice your behaviour, and invite yourself back into making a choice, one tiny moment at a time.

Me Moment: *Pick one small action today and pause. Ask yourself: Is this habit or free will? If it's a choice you still love or deem necessary, celebrate it. If it's a stale habit, make a gentle shift.*

Day 66: Play with Possibility

When you approach life with curiosity, everything softens. Obstacles start looking like invitations. Habits start looking like experiments. You begin flexing your creative muscle and seeing how many paths there actually are. Most limits are learned. Possibility is a practice.

Me Moment: *Choose one area of your life today—your morning routine, your lunch break, your evening wind-down—and ask, What's another way I could do this? Maybe it's swapping coffee for a walk. Maybe it's writing one page in your journal instead of scrolling on your phone. Try one tiny switch. This doesn't have to be permanent. Just a willingness to get comfortable with shaking things up and flexing your "possibility muscle" from time to time.*

Day 67: Curiosity Over Criticism

When something doesn't go the way you hoped, the habit is often to critique yourself: *Why did I do that? What's wrong with me?* But curiosity is the antidote. It lifts you out of judgement and into learning. It opens doors instead of slamming them shut. Imagine how much softer life would feel if you started meeting yourself with wonder instead of war!

Me Moment: *If you catch yourself criticizing something you did or didn't do today, pause. Ask instead, What can I learn about myself here? Even one moment of curiosity over criticism builds a new, freer, softer way of being.*

Day 68: The Winding Way

It's tempting to want guarantees before you act. Will this make me money? Will it be worth my time? Will it lead somewhere impressive? But curiosity doesn't come with a business plan. Growth isn't always efficient or strategic. It's often messy, surprising, and full of detours that shape you in ways you can't predict. Take the pressure off to map out the whole journey. Trust the nudge and take one small step.

Me Moment: *Think of one idea, project, or nudge that's been tugging at you. Now, write down all the ways you've tried to organise it, optimize it, or force it into a long-term plan. Then, cross it out. Underneath, write a simple question, What would feel fun, easy, or energizing to try next? Just one step. That's all curiosity is asking for.*

Day 69: The Bridge

Think of curiosity as a bridge between where you are now and where life is calling you. It doesn't always lead to a clear outcome, but it *always* leads somewhere. Curiosity is a mystical force, a gentle tug from deep within. When we try to make it make sense too soon, we could end up steering ourselves back onto the same old road instead of following the one opening up ahead. Maybe this isn't *the* thing, but maybe it's the thing that wakes something else up, and it becomes a stepping stone that leads to what's next.

Me Moment: *Today, intentionally follow one random spark. Ask a new question. Wander a different aisle. Pick up a book you normally wouldn't. Notice how it opens something in you—a window, a possibility, a breath of fresh air. You're not here to chase a result or get your hopes up. You're simply here to show your intuition that you're listening.*

Day 70: The Curiosity Effect

You've spent the last few weeks letting your curiosity crack the door open to new experiences, new urges, and new possibilities. Maybe you followed a tiny nudge. Maybe you noticed how often you second-guess yourself. Maybe you said yes to something without needing to know exactly where it would lead. That's how change happens. It's not always loud. It's often a whisper—and you heard it.

Me Moment: *In what ways has curiosity softened, expanded, or brightened your daily life? What small shift are you most proud of?*

Day 71

Hide and Seek

You are not here to be like everyone else. You're here to be fully alive. To be electric. To be your favourite version of yourself—unique, real, radiant.

You are a multidimensional being. Some facets of you are probably easier to access than others: the caretaker, the achiever, the responsible one. And then there are parts you've tucked away: the fierce, the sexy, the silly, the free. There may have been a point when you learned those pieces weren't "safe" to show. Maybe someone told you. Maybe the world modeled it. But now? These facets are ready to come forward and show you what you're made of.

Today and the next few weeks are about dropping the mask—noticing when you slip into old roles, investigating who you really are underneath them, and taking small but brave steps toward letting your real self lead.

Me Moment: *Close your eyes and ask, What part of me have I been hiding—and why? Let the answer rise without judgement. Sit with her presence for a moment. Let her know she's welcome. Now imagine this one facet of you greatly enhanced—that's your alter ego.*

FAVOURITE SELF

Day 72: The Myth of Your "Best" Self

During this journey, you may fall into the trap of believing you have to become some "perfect" version of yourself—fully healed, fully evolved, endlessly radiant—as if there is a personal development pinnacle. Even personal growth can start to feel like a performance. But your Favourite Self isn't on the other side of a finish line you cross. She's not the most perfectly healed, productive, or impressive version of you. She's the most *alive* version, the most *you*. Let go of the myth that you need to be "better." You are already whole, and the real work is becoming more *you*.

Me Moment: *Today, make two lists. First, list the qualities you feel when you're most alive, connected, and yourself. Second, list the traits you believe you're "supposed" to have to be your best or highest self. Compare them. Which ones feel real and which ones feel like expectations you've outgrown? Notice what your soul is craving more of.*

Day 73: Destination Unknown

What once felt important will change and evolve just like the seasons. What once felt like the *exact* version of you and the life you craved might not fit anymore. Suffering can happen when we attach to an outcome or expectation and become unwilling to shift.

Me Moment: *Where have you been trying to stay the same out of habit, pressure, or fear? Write down one area of your life where you're ready to give yourself permission to change into something that feels even more you—whether it's a rhythm, a dream, or a definition of who you are. Let this serve as an ongoing reminder that even the most expansive and dreamiest of visions need room to grow, shift, fade, and transform.*

Day 74: Alter Ego

On Day 71, you met your alter ego. She's an integral part of your Favourite Self, but the one that needs most coaxing. Now, it's time to get curious. When does she show up? Is it when you're goofing off with loved ones? Dropping into the zone at the gym? Speaking passionately?

Me Moment: *Today, deepen your relationship with her by reflecting on these prompts: When do I feel her stir? When do I pull her back? Where does she live in my body? What is the essence she is inviting me to claim more fully?*

Day 75: Key to the Cage

There's a difference between who you truly are and who you're expected to be. The question is: Where did those expectations come from? Family, culture, social media, school, an old version of you? Most of the "shoulds" you carry weren't chosen—they were inherited. Now you get to ask, *Which ones still fit? And which feel like cages you're ready to step out of?*

Me Moment: *Pick one trait from your "supposed to be" list that feels heavy or false. Ask yourself, Who told me this was necessary to be worthy or lovable? What might my life feel like if I didn't hold myself to their standard anymore? Let yourself imagine a little more freedom.*

Day 76: The Flare

Right before you level up, the old patterns fight hard to pull you back. Doubt creeps in. Resistance flares. Habits you thought you'd outgrown start whispering again. Most people mistake this for a warning sign: *Maybe I'm not ready. Maybe I should back off.* But it's not a warning—it's a threshold. The only way to step into your bigger life is to move through it.

Me Moment: *Today, reflect on the following questions: Where am I feeling the pull to contract back into old ways? What would it look like to use this as an opportunity to repattern and choose again, choose anew?*

Day 77: The Unfolding

Parts of you that were once hidden, hushed, or waiting are beginning to come forward. You're beginning to experience yourself in a new way—more open, complete, and truer. This is the process of unfolding, of meeting yourself with clarity instead of critique, presence instead of pressure. It's a return to who you've been all along.

Me Moment: *What's one part of yourself you're starting to trust more? Is there a side of you that now feels safe or exciting to share with others?*

Day 78: Call her forward

Many performing artists, like Beyoncé with her alter ego Sasha Fierce, have shared how they tap into a bold, embodied version of themselves when stepping into something intimidating. They don't fake it. They *become* it. They project that essence forward and let her lead. The point isn't to turn life into a performance, but rather to know you have this inner diva power within you when you need her!

Me Moment: *Take a moment to connect with the fierce, grounded, magnetic, or fully expressed version of you. Close your eyes and imagine her clearly. How does she move? What does she know? Now answer the following: In what areas of your life would it help to call her forward? What's something coming up, big or small, where her presence could shift the energy? And what might she be here to teach you?*

Day 79: Walking Contradiction

During the journey to becoming your Favourite Self, you might feel the urge to make her make sense—to line everything up neatly, to fit her into a box with tidy categories and labels.

But you are not a product. You are a wildly complex, deeply nuanced, ever-evolving being. As you bring your Favourite Self forward, resist the temptation to box her in again. Let her be bold and tender . . . or quiet and electric . . . or fierce and nurturing. You're allowed to be a living, breathing contradiction.

Me Moment: *Notice where you're trying to simplify or water yourself down to be more "understandable." Then name two traits you love that seem to be opposites of each other. Feel them coexisting within you and let that be okay.*

FAVOURITE SELF

Day 80: Right vs. Happy

Yes, we all want to be both right *and* happy—but sometimes, the deeper power comes from knowing you don't have to prove anything at all. Your Favourite Self knows when to stand firm and when to walk away. She knows her worth doesn't depend on being understood or agreed with. And as long as no one's getting hurt you're allowed to let someone be wrong. If they want to argue that $1 + 1 = 3$, fine. Your peace is more important.

Me Moment: *Think of a moment where you felt the urge to correct, explain, or defend your point. What would it feel like to simply let it go? Not because you're giving up, but because you're choosing yourself. Today, walk away when it protects your peace. That's not weakness. It's self-respect.*

Day 81: Just for You

Dedicating a space to the beautiful life you are creating—a drawer, a shelf, a small altar—is a powerful act of devotion. It's a way to honour what you're building, who you're becoming, and what makes you feel most like yourself. This isn't about making something pretty or perfect. It's about choosing to make it meaningful.

Me Moment: *Set aside a small space for your Favourite Self. It could be a drawer, a tray, a basket, or a tiny shrine. Fill it with a few items that speak to the essence you're claiming more fully. Let it be personal, evolving, and just for you—a place that holds your vision and reminds you of who you truly are.*

Day 82: In it Together

The way you experience your body shapes how fully you show up. It's in the way you hold yourself, nourish yourself, speak to yourself. It's not about how your body looks—but how deeply you let yourself *live* inside it.

Me Moment: *Stand in front of a mirror and place a hand over your heart or on a part of your body you've struggled to love. Say, This is the body my Favourite Self lives in. Breathe into it. Let this reverence remind you to show up for your body with devotion and self-respect.*

Day 83: Little Love Notes

Healing isn't just the hard stuff—tears, breakthroughs, deep work. It also happens through joy—laughter, lightness, play, and celebration. The good moments aren't just a break from the work—they *are* the work. Celebration anchors growth. It tells your system, *This is safe, this is real, do more of this.*

Me Moment: *Write a love note to yourself starting with the sentence, Here's how I showed up for myself this week . . . Be specific and recognize what's unfolding.*

Day 84: Witness Your Becoming

Bringing your Favourite Self to the surface is now in motion—a steady accumulation of brave, beautiful choices. Notice the changes: when you softened instead of spiraled, stayed open instead of shut down, or let your spark shine.

Me Moment: *Finish this sentence without disclaimers, without minimizing: I'm so proud of myself for . . .*

Phase Two: Let's Play

If Phase One was about waking up to your spark, Phase Two is about giving it air. This is where you'll loosen the grip on doing things "right" and begin experimenting with what feels alive. The goal isn't to fake positivity or chase transformation—it's to get curious, try things on, and notice what lights you up. You'll start to build trust in your inner knowing by following the threads of joy and noticing how good it feels to let them lead.

Days 85 to 98 invite you to explore style and space as tools for self-expression. Clothes, surroundings, and the small details of daily life become ways to mirror the energy you want more of.

In Days 99 to 112, you'll start breaking the rules that never really fit you—the ones that told you to water yourself down, to perform, to be smaller than you are. You'll begin reclaiming the traits you once fought so hard to "fix" as sources of power.

Days 113 to 126 are all about flirting with life: practicing awe, savouring small pleasures, and letting yourself be wooed by the world around you.

Next, in Days 127 to 140, you'll stop asking if what you create is "good" and start noticing how creativity already pulses through your daily life. Once you open yourself to that flow, new possibilities emerge, and everyday life feels more satisfying.

Days 141 to 154 shake up the ruts—not with dramatic reinventions, but with tiny rebellions and everyday disruptions that bring more honesty and ease into your routines.

Finally, Days 155 to 180 help you tune into your essence—that distinct frequency that is uniquely yours. You'll practice calling it forward in small, embodied ways until it feels less like something you have to think about and more like your natural state.

Phase Two is about giving yourself permission to be curious. Let's get messy. Let's make it fun. Let's play.

Day 85
Costume Change

Society wants us to think that style is shallow, that it is about impressing others, dressing for a role, or following rules. But true style? It's liberation. It's a magnet. It's a way to say, *this is who I am* and, *this is the life I'm calling in*. A tool like that can be very dangerous to a system that benefits from keeping you small and disconnected from your inner knowing.

We're reclaiming style as a tool for self-expression, not performance, perfection, or pressure. You'll explore what style means for *you*—and how getting dressed can become a daily act of devotion, artistry, and delight.

Style is a story you tell without saying a word. But whose story are you telling? Many of us dress in a way that makes us blend in, live up to an expectation, or stay acceptable. We don't even realize it's a costume—chosen to protect or adhere. Today is about getting curious: If you've been dressing to hide aspects of yourself to fit a certain role, then what version of you is being hidden underneath?

Me Moment: *Stand in front of your closet. Do your clothing choices feel like you or like you are dressing to fit an expectation? What feels like armor? What feels like a mask? What would your closet look like if you decided to dress from a place of freedom instead of performance?*

Day 86: It Was Never About Pink

Pink has never been just a colour. It's long been a symbol of femininity—and for many of us, something we were taught to turn away from. Somewhere along the way, you may have learned that embracing your feminine energy was a liability. Today is about noticing what you've been taught to reject and why. Maybe "girly" felt frivolous, weak, or not for someone like you. Maybe you learned to roll your eyes at glamour or softness because the world convinced you it was less powerful. But rejecting something doesn't always make you free. Sometimes, it keeps you boxed in by limiting your options.

Me Moment: *Think about something traditionally feminine, whether it's a colour, accessory, or vibe you've long dismissed. Ask, What story did I attach to it? Is that story still true? You don't have to reclaim it, you don't have to like it—but you do deserve to understand your resistance.*

Day 87: Inner Child Delight

Today, you're getting dressed to delight the gaze of your inner child. To signal that she still belongs here. That her giddiness, imagination, and boldness still matter. You don't have to recreate childhood outfits (unless you want to, of course). The invitation is to dress in a way that would have made her light up; a colour she loved, a playful pattern, a texture she couldn't stop touching, or maybe it's just a small detail—a sticker on your water bottle, a swipe of glitter, a charm on your shoe. Go all in or keep it subtle. The point is to acknowledge her.

Me Moment: *Today, dress with her in mind. Ask, What would she smile at? Then wear it like a reunion. She's still here and she's paying attention. Practicing this, whether it's daily or once in a while, can be a delightful lifeline back to the version of you who knew how to feel joy without permission. It's more healing than it might seem.*

Day 88: Dress for the Life You Want

The more often you dress as your Favourite Self, the easier it is to access her. Think of clothing as an entry point—each choice is a thread that weaves your inner and outer worlds closer together until it feels like total congruence. When your inner and outer worlds start to match, you unlock a subtle kind of magnetism — a radiance that draws people in, not because you're trying, but because you're true. And, my goodness, does the world need more realness!

Me Moment: *Yesterday, you dressed to delight your inner child. Today, we are taking it one step further. Start thinking about what it would look like to dress for the life you want to live—not necessarily for the roles you want to step into, but for the energy you want to experience more of. How can your choices reflect that energy right now? Let your style be a sneak peek of the life you're calling in.*

Day 89: The Energy of Colour

What if your closet was more than just fabric and form, but a portal to healing, alignment, and intention? According to the traditional chakra system, every colour carries a frequency—a whisper to your body, a nudge to your soul. When you get dressed with colour in mind, you're not just choosing clothes, you're choosing how you want to feel: red for rootedness, orange for pleasure and creativity, yellow for confidence and vitality, green for love and abundance, blue for truth and communication, indigo for intuition, or violet for sacred connection.

Me Moment: *What do you want to heal or enhance today? Scan your closet and choose a colour based on what your spirit is craving. Try wearing the same colour, in some form or fashion, for a week in different ways and see what unfolds.*

Day 90: Adorn, Don't Perform

Is it preference or performance? Am I dressing for the trend? For the male gaze? For approval—of the boss, the other moms, the powers that be? Let's pivot. Style isn't a performance—it's a love note to your spirit. A visual conversation with your Favourite Self. You get to play with how you frame it. You have the power to make choices with intention, *How do I want to feel today—and how can I reflect that on the outside?*

Me Moment: *Today, take a moment to notice the intention behind how you get dressed. Is it jewellry—or are you decorating yourself? Is it makeup—or is it art? Is it just an outfit—or your chosen expression for the day? There's no right answer here—just perspective. But the mindset behind it changes everything. When you shift from performing to expressing, from covering up to adorning, style becomes something you do for yourself, not for approval.*

Day 91: Your Sacred Style

You've just spent several days exploring style not as a surface-level game, but as a sacred act of self-expression. You've tried things on. Let things go. Gotten playful. So, what has shifted?

Me Moment: *Take a moment to reflect on what this exploration into style unlocked for you. What did you learn about yourself through getting dressed with intention? What resistance softened? What desires were revealed?*

Day 92: Style Your Space

Like your wardrobe, your home is also a mirror. It reflects what you value, how you feel, and who you believe yourself to be. Style isn't just about what you wear, it's also found in what you surround yourself with. The textures, colors, objects, and energy in your physical space can either dull your spirit or wake it up. Look around; if your space were speaking to you, what would it say? Would it whisper comfort, creativity, aliveness? Or would it nudge you gently, asking for more beauty, more intention, more you?

Me Moment: *Today, don't change anything—just observe. Walk through your home with fresh eyes, as if you were a guest visiting for the first time. What story does each room tell about you? What corners or objects feel alive, and which feel stagnant? Simply notice, without fixing.*

Day 93: Unspoken Messages

The objects you use every day can subtly—or not so subtly—impact your well-being and even reaffirm old beliefs. The chipped mug, the pile of mail, the décor you never really liked—each one reflects something back to you. Are they affirming comfort, care, and vitality? Or are they echoing patterns of neglect, scarcity, or "not good enough"? Your space tells a story, whether or not you've chosen it.

Me Moment: *Look at the everyday objects around you—the ones you touch, see, or move past without thinking. What messages are they sending? Choose one item and ask: What belief is this reflecting back to me? If it feels outdated, what could take its place?*

Day 94: Make It Yours

A home comes alive when it carries your fingerprints—those little touches that only you could choose. A bowl of seashells you collected, a rock from a favourite hike, a sketch you drew, a quirky thrift-store find—these small gestures turn a house into a reflection of you. They remind you, and anyone who walks in, that this space is lived in by someone with spirit, history, and heart.

Me Moment: *Add one personal touch to your space today. It could be something you already own, something from nature, or something you stumble upon that feels exactly right. Place it somewhere visible. Let it be a reminder that this is your space; it supports your essence and holds your dreams.*

Day 95: Colour Your Space

Just as colour in your wardrobe influences your energy, so does colour in your home. Soft blues can soothe, bold reds can energize, greens can bring balance, and yellows can spark joy. Surrounding yourself with intentional colors invites your space to support your mood and overall outlook.

Me Moment: *Look around at the colors in one room. What mood do they create? What mood do you want to feel there? Add or change something—a blanket, a candle, a print—that aligns with the energy you want.*

Day 96: Clear the Static

A cluttered space can drain your energy. The mess doesn't just sit there; it hums in the background of your mind. When you clear a stagnant area, you aren't just "tidying up," you are unblocking flow. When your environment is lighter, you are too.

Me Moment: Choose one small area—a drawer, a shelf, or a stack of papers—and clear it. As you do, imagine you're also clearing a little stagnancy in yourself. Notice how the shift in your space shifts you.

Day 97: Sensory Atmosphere

Home isn't just what you see, it's what you *feel*. Scent, sound, and texture shape your experience just as much as décor. A playlist, a favourite scent, the feel of soft sheets—all of these are style, too. They set the tone for how you live inside your space.

Me Moment: Today, tune in to the sensory layers of your home. Add or adjust one thing—a song, a scent, a cozy texture—that feels like your Favourite Self. Notice how quickly your nervous system responds.

Day 98: Your Sacred Surroundings

Over the past week, you've explored how your home reflects you—what you've outgrown, what uplifts you, and how small changes can transform how you feel.

Me Moment: Reflect on what you learned by bringing more intention to your surroundings. What felt freeing? What resistance came up? How can you continue letting your space be a mirror of your Favourite Self?

Day 99
Mixed Messages

We all hit a point in our lives when we are taught to shrink. Maybe not directly—but through a sideways comment, a classroom rule, a glance that said, "Tone it down." You learned which parts of yourself to quiet. You edited your essence, your ideas, your dreams. Bit by bit, you started believing that was maturity. That dimming yourself was the price of being taken seriously.

In this stretch, you'll notice the stories you've internalized—about being too sensitive, too weird, too *you*, not enough of this, too much of that. You'll learn to flip them into clues. You'll start playing with what it feels like to stop editing. To let the real you take up space. To wear, like a badge, the parts you once masked.

Over time, many of us absorbed messages like, "You're, too loud, too emotional, too ambitious," and more. Then, just as confusingly, "You're not enough." It's dizzying. These messages aren't facts—they're old stories—and you're allowed to set them down. It's time to become ungovernable in the best way.

Me Moment: *Make two lists today:*

1. *Times or traits you've felt* too much.
2. *Times or traits you've felt* not enough.

Look at them side by side. How many of these contradictions have you internalized? Which ones still carry weight? Now ask, Are these even true? Or are they just internalized echoes? Notice what you've been carrying and consider what you're ready to put down.

Day 100: The Good Girl Glitch

Be nice. Don't interrupt. Smile more. Don't take up too much space. Be easy to love. Maybe you learned that being "good" meant being small, soft and predictable. That likeability was the prize, and your full self was the risk, but let's be honest, have those rules made you feel free?

Me Moment: *Think about the rules you've followed to be seen as "good" or praise-worthy. Then think about breaking one of those rules on purpose. This might look like: saying no when you usually say yes, speaking up when you'd normally stay quiet, or skipping the thank-you text if it's just to be polite. As you visualize yourself breaking a rule, notice what it brings up in your body, notice how the inner critic pushes back. What is she scared of? For today, we are just noticing, and that's enough.*

Day 101: Permission Slip

The old rules say you have to earn fun. That you need to prove you're responsible before you're allowed to let loose. But those rules aren't true—and they never were. You're allowed to be serious about your dreams and still wear glitter on your face. You're allowed to hold heavy things and still laugh at dumb jokes. You're allowed to be a grown person who plays. You don't need anyone's permission to break those old rules—but in case it helps, you have it anyway.

Me Moment: *Write yourself a permission slip: I, [your name], officially grant myself permission to _______. Let the blank be something playful. Something freeing. Something delightfully you.*

Day 102: Claim It

We all have a dream so bold it feels safer to hide. Maybe you tucked it away because someone said it was selfish, unrealistic, or that you don't have what it takes. But that calling wasn't planted in you by accident— it's meant for you. When you bring it back into the light, you bring back possibility.

Me Moment: *Think of one bold dream you've buried. Say it out loud, even if it scares you. Let yourself hear the sound of your own voice naming it. You don't have to act on it yet. Today is about giving it air.*

Day 103: Try It On Anyway

Parts of yourself may have gone underground over the years—not because they weren't real, but because they felt risky to show. Maybe it's a boldness you watered down, a sensitivity you muted, or a quirk you downplayed. Those parts are still alive in you, waiting to be let out. What happens when you let a hidden quality step forward, even just for today? Think of it less as a declaration and more as an experiment.

Me Moment: *Choose one quality you've muted. Instead of hiding it, channel it through your body today. Move, speak, or dress in a way that lets this trait rise to the surface. Notice what happens when you stop fighting it and start owning it.*

Day 104: The Shape of Your Love

Right now, as a mother, you are creating the mold for your kids. The way you respond to your kids' big feelings, the tone you use when they mess up, the way you praise them or pressure them—it all becomes part of their inner world. Does your love say they need to earn rest? That they're too much? Or does it say you are safe here, you are celebrated, you are already whole.

Me Moment: Get honest with yourself: How is your parenting shaping the ones you love? Where might your words, tone, or expectations be mirroring a mold you're ready to break? Name one pattern you don't want to pass on—and one new way you want your love to feel in your home today.

Day 105: A Little Different

You've been cracking open old stories, holding them to the light, and asking *is this even mine?* That's big work. Today, notice what feels different now that you've seen the mold you've been trying to fit into?

Me Moment: Reflect on these questions: What discoveries have you made? What are you no longer willing to shrink for? And what are you willing to expand?

Day 106: Rewrite the Label

Labels are like name tags you didn't ask for. At some point, someone slapped one on you—too sensitive, too assertive, too loud—and you started to wear it like it was yours—but you get to peel it off. You get to write a new one in your own handwriting.

Me Moment: *Choose one label you've carried that never felt like it was true or accurate. Now rewrite it, not as a soft reframe, but as a proclamation. For example:*

- *"Too sensitive"* → *"Deeply attuned"*
- *"Too assertive"* → *"Powerful and present"*
- *"Too loud"* → *"Unapologetically expressive"*

Now speak it out loud. Try it on for size.

Day 107: Take Up Space

Taking up space isn't necessarily about being bold or loud. Sometimes it's quiet, subtle, still. It's resting when others keep going. Asking a question when everyone's nodding. Doing things differently and not explaining why. Every time you let yourself show up fully, without pulling back or rushing to please or prove, you're building a reality that says it's safe to be me.

Me Moment: *Choose one small way to take up space your way today. Maybe it's wearing something expressive, asking for what you need, or saying no without guilt. Maybe it's pausing before reacting. Check in with your body before and after. How does it feel to be fully in your lane, no edits?*

Day 108: Are You Okay?

How often do you shape your choices around how others might respond—seeking approval, avoiding discomfort, trying not to disappoint? It's a habit many of us carry, especially if we've been conditioned to prioritize others' feelings over our own. But living a peaceful life means being willing to disappoint someone else in order to protect one's own clarity, comfort, or happiness. That can feel hard, even unnatural, when you've spent a lifetime trying to make everyone else okay first.

Me Moment: *Think of a moment when you hesitated to act, speak, or express because of how someone might react. Now flip the script: What did you feel? What did you need? What truth wanted to come through? Today, let your own reaction be the compass. You are allowed to trust yourself first.*

Day 109: Your Living Guidelines

You've spent time letting go of the rules that were handed to you. Now it's time to write the agreements you truly want to live by. Think of them as promises to yourself, a personal code that supports who you are and how you want to move through the world.

Examples might sound like:

- *I promise to never subdue my joy to make others comfortable.*

- *I promise to always speak to myself with kindness.*

Me Moment: *Write your own living guidelines. Begin each line with I promise to always . . . or I promise to never . . . Let these become touchstones you can return to whenever you need reminding of who you choose to be.*

Day 110: A Declaration for Motherhood

Motherhood can pull you in a thousand directions. But at the centre of it all is you—the anchor your family looks to. Taking care of yourself isn't separate from being a good mum; it's what allows you to show up with love and presence.

Me Moment: *Write a declaration that guides you in motherhood. Begin with As a mother, I . . . and let the words flow. Maybe yours sounds like: As a mother, I honour my needs so my children learn to honour theirs. As a mother, I hold space for joy—for them and for me. Keep it as a reminder that your well-being is part of the story you're writing with your family*

Day 111: Break Character

Sometimes, we get stuck in a feeling. Not because it's true, but because we've committed to a role: The Resentful One, The Martyr, The One Who's Always Fine, etc. We use that role as armor. We pick a lane and then we forget we can move out of it. But you can *always* break character. Even mid-scene—even mid-sentence. You can go from sullen to silly, from icy to warm, from tense to soft. You don't owe anyone any kind of justification. You don't have to explain the pivot. Just trust that you're allowed to choose again—over and over.

Me Moment: *Think of a moment recently where you felt stuck in a mood, an identity, or a reaction that didn't feel good. If it's happening now, even better. Ask: What role am I playing here? Is this really who I want to be? Now try this; take a breath, shake your arms out, make a sound, move your face, do something that snaps you out of that character; then choose a new one. Even if it's just for the next five minutes, even if no one else understands the change. This is your scene to rewrite.*

Day 112: Break Free

You've unlearned, reclaimed, and remembered who you were before editing yourself. You broke the mold in quiet ways and bold ones. That deserves to be celebrated.

Me Moment: *Light a candle. Play a song that stirs something within you. Smile at yourself in the mirror. Then ask: What did I break free from? What truth did I reclaim? What part of me feels more alive now?*

Day 113

More Awe, Please

The universe is always flirting with you. Through timing, glimmers, and ideas that tug at your sleeve or little winks inviting you to lean closer. It's a relationship. A quiet exchange. Like making eye contact with a moment. Like showing up as if life itself is a date worth dressing up for.

In this section, you'll tune into life's love notes. You'll flirt with life. You'll experiment with presence, pleasure, charm, and self-devotion, because feeling lit up changes how you move through the world. When you let your inner spark show, life responds. Not because you're chasing anything, but because you're finally open to receiving what's already been reaching for you.

At some point, awe became rare. Life got busy, routine, rushed, but awe is one of the most transformative states we can access. It reminds us that we're part of something bigger. It softens the edges of everyday life and connects us to wonder. Awe isn't something that happens *to* you, it happens *from* you. It's your response to the way light bends on the floor, the harmony of trees moving in unison, the feeling in your chest when a lyric hits just right. It's not about chasing magic, it's about noticing the wonder woven into the everyday.

Me Moment: *Today, practice awe-spotting. When something stirs even the tiniest "whoa," pause and breathe with it. Let yourself soften. Awe reconnects you to what's real—and to what's worth paying attention to.*

Day 114: Romance the Moment

You don't need a partner, candles, or a getaway to feel swept away. Romance lives in how you *experience* a moment. Slowing down. Noticing the texture. Adding a little "extra" just because it delights you. This is how you shift from going through life to dancing with it.

Me Moment: *Pick one ordinary part of your day: grocery shopping, taking a walk, getting yourself ready for the day. Then, add something extra: a little sashay, perfume, music in your earbuds, a favourite fabric, or mood lighting while you get dressed. Do it like it's a scene from a movie. Not for anyone else. Don't wait for enchantment, make it!*

Day 115: Witty Banter

Imagine being in a flirtatious relationship with life. The blooms. The breeze. The squirrels chasing each other like they're in a rom-com. The killer sunset. The unexpected kindness. That's the universe showing off—leaving little love notes everywhere. Maybe it's time to start winking back.

Me Moment: *Today, have a little witty banter with life. Say things like, "Okay, Earth. I see you. Show me how cute you are." When something delights you, even just a glimmer, respond. Smile. Say, "thank you." Whisper, "Oh, you did that for me?" Make it a game. Follow the fun. Give yourself permission to be wooed by the moment.*

Day 116: The Vibe You Bring

Your presence carries power. The vibe you bring into a space doesn't just affect how others experience you—it shapes how *you* experience the moment, too. Every room, conversation, or transition is a chance to choose between moving on autopilot or showing up with purpose.

Me Moment: *Before you enter your next space—your kitchen, a meeting, a text thread—pause and ask: What vibe am I bringing with me? What energy do I want to radiate? Choose with intention. Let it be a small act of alignment.*

Day 117: This Is for Me

You don't have to earn pleasure. You don't have to justify delight. You are allowed to do things just because they light you up. When you choose something simply because it's for *you,* you send a message to life, and to your nervous system: *I matter. My joy matters.*

Me Moment: *Today, do something that feels good simply because it's for you. Maybe it's a favourite song on repeat, a slow stretch, or using the "fancy" version of something just because you want to. As you do it, say to yourself,* This is for me. *Feel the meaning of that. Let it sink into your system as a powerful act of self-honouring. You're allowed.*

Day 118: Let It In

Life is already loving you. In small ways, constantly, but when you've spent years on alert—waiting, pushing, proving—it's easy to miss the signs; or to mistrust them. The work now isn't to earn more love; it's to *let in* what's already here.

Me Moment: *Today, practice letting it land. Receive the compliment. Joyfully accept the help. Savour the small things that feed you—a nourishing snack, sunlight on your skin, a deep breath that feels like yours. No deflecting. No justifying. Just say, "Thank you." Breathe it in. Let life love you, and let it be safe to be nourished by what you receive.*

Day 119: Flirty Little Life

You've softened. Not in a small way but in an open, magnetic, I'm-in-a-relationship-with-life kind of way. You've noticed beauty, said yes to presence, and let yourself be delighted. That's big stuff! Because when you stop pushing joy away, you attract more of it.

Me Moment: *Reflect on and celebrate what has shifted this week. Write it down. Let it be proof that life flirts with you—and you're finally flirting back.*

Day 120: Let Them See You Sparkle

When you let others witness your lightness, silliness, and play, you're modelling something radical: it's safe to be fully alive. As a parent, this matters more than you think. You're showing your kids that adulthood doesn't mean burnout, that being responsible doesn't mean being unhappy. Your sparkle gives them permission to keep theirs.

Me Moment: *Today, let your kids see you in a playful moment. A kitchen dance. A made-up song. Losing your mind over the beautiful sunset or full bloom. Don't force their participation, and don't dim yourself if they tease you. Let them see that your joy isn't performative—it's who you are.*

Day 121: Lock Screen Magic

Your Favourite Self has an energetic signature—a colour, a texture, a feeling. And like anything alive, it can evolve over time. But giving it form, even for a moment, helps you stay connected to it. When you place that energy in your daily visual field, it becomes a quiet, steady reminder of what you're claiming for yourself.

Me Moment: *Choose a colour that feels like your Favourite Self right now. Set it as your phone's lock screen or background, something you'll see frequently throughout your day. Each time it catches your eye let it cue you to tune back into your vibrancy.*

Day 122: Flirt Like You Mean It

Flirting is an energy, a magnetic mix of charm, presence, and play. It's warmth without pressure. Seduction without expectation. It's the sparkle in your eye when you feel good just being you. When you flirt with life, you create a rhythm of delight, of showing up with just enough mischief to make the moment shimmer.

Me Moment: *Today, flirt with your life. Get dressed like the day is lucky to have you. Make eye contact with your reflection and say, "You're kind of amazing." Let your Favourite Self take the lead and add a little flirtatious energy to everything you do.*

Day 123: Choose You

There's flirting and then there's chasing approval—over-explaining your choices to seem agreeable, smart, or not intimidating. Constantly wondering, *Did I do enough? Was I too much? Do they still like me?* But here's the truth: chasing doesn't earn love—it just exhausts you. Choosing yourself means catching those moments in which you chase approval and choosing differently. It means trusting your worth, even without applause. No one else's approval will ever feel as good as your own.

Me Moment: *Think of a recent moment when you felt yourself chasing approval. What did it look like? What did it feel like in your body? Now ask yourself, What would it have looked like to choose myself instead? Today, catch just one of those moments mid-chase—and pivot. Even a small shift counts. A pause. A breath. A decision made from self-trust, not fear.*

Day 124: Make Life Blush

Sensuality is about presence. It's about tuning into all five senses—touch, taste, smell, sound, sight—and letting the world reach you. When you move through life that way, even the simplest moments become richer.

Me Moment: *Today, choose one moment and experience it with all five senses. Let your presence turn the ordinary into something intimate.*

Day 125: Energy Check

Your Favourite Self isn't perfect— she's the most honest version of you. When you embody her, life responds differently—not because you're trying harder, but because you're more nourished, more whole, more *you*.

Me Moment: *Today, check in with your body. What does your Favourite Self radiate when she's flirting with life? What's her pace, her breath, her tone, her rhythm? How does she nourish herself— through movement, words, or rest? Move, speak, and choose as her. Even if it's just for one hour.*

Day 126: Love Story

These past two weeks have been an invitation to remember what's already here—presence, play, and awe. When you begin to pay attention, life reveals itself as more connected, more charming, more alive. It starts to feel like a love story between you and life, and between you and yourself.

Me Moment: *Look back on the past two weeks. What delighted you? What surprised you? What shifted when you got a little flirty? Write it down. Celebrate it. Keep the spark alive.*

Day 127

When Did It Start Feeling Like Work?

You were never *not* creative. You just learned to question it. Maybe someone told you your creation wasn't "good." Maybe it got graded, judged, ignored. Maybe you started believing creativity belonged to other people—people with training, skill, or time. But creativity isn't about talent or recognition. It's a life force. A sacred expression of your inner world. It's the part of you that shapes meaning, makes beauty, and turns the unseen into something felt.

This section is about unlearning the pressure to be impressive and remembering how to create—not just art, but life. You'll follow inspiration instead of perfection, make space for mess, and notice how creativity already pulses through your daily life—in how you speak, move, solve, love, and show up. You'll reclaim your right to create something just because it feels good. You'll stop asking if it's good enough, and start asking, *does it feel like me?*

Our culture loves to sort people into categories. You are either "artistic" or you aren't. But those labels create false limits, and a lot of us learned to believe them. Creativity isn't relegated to the arts. It's how you solve problems, how you dress, how you tell a story, or rearrange a room. It's not a talent; it's a flow—one that belongs to everyone. And yet, many of us lost our connection to it the moment it started being graded, judged, or monetized. It stopped being play and started being work.

Me Moment: *Think about where creativity started feeling complicated for you. Then name one or two ways you already use creativity in your life today. Maybe it's the way you pack your kids' lunches, the way you help solve problems at work, or the way you put together an outfit.*

Day 128: The Lost Art of Not Caring

At some point, doing something "just for fun" stopped feeling like enough. If you weren't good at it, why bother? But that mindset is the death of creativity. You don't need to be great at something to get something great *from* it. Freedom lives in showing up because something in you wants to. In being seen trying. In following what feels right, even if it's clumsy, awkward, or unfinished. That willingness *is* the art. That's what makes it yours.

Me Moment: *Today, let yourself be a beginner. Draw. Sing. Write a poem that makes no sense. Let it be silly. Let it be fun. Let it remind you: you're allowed to be creative without being perfect.*

Day 129: Unfinished Business

All those half-written stories, forgotten sketchbooks, abandoned ideas—they weren't failures; they were sparks, experiments, evidence of your curiosity. We've been conditioned to believe that unless something is seen all the way through—polished, perfected, praised—it doesn't count. But what if following a whim or diving into a creative rabbit hole *without* finishing is still worthy? You're allowed to start things simply because they light you up. To move on when they don't. Explore for the thrill of it and then let go.

Me Moment: *Today, think of a creative project you started but never finished. Instead of judging it, thank it. What did it give you at the time—relief, excitement, distraction, joy? Let go of the need to complete it, and instead honour what it sparked in you. Sometimes it really is about the journey and not the finished product.*

Day 130: Blast from the Past

When you think about something you used to love—playing dress up, making up dances, decorating, baking, climbing trees—you may zero in on how good you were at it or what came of it. But what lit you up wasn't the result. It was the *feeling*, the freedom you felt, how present you were, and the way time disappeared. That's what you're being called to reconnect with—not a hobby, but a frequency.

Me Moment: *Today, pick one creative thing you used to enjoy, even if it's been years. Ask yourself: What did I actually love about it? Was it the focus, the play, the physicality, the solitude? Let yourself name the feeling—that's the part worth reclaiming.*

Day 131: Perfection as Protection

Perfectionism isn't just about high standards; it's often about safety. If you perfect it, you won't be judged. If you keep it to yourself, no one can reject it. But protection can turn into a cage. Creativity needs air, risk, vulnerability. It needs your imperfections, your humanness.

Me Moment: *Notice where perfectionism might be keeping you safe but also holding you back. What do you fear would happen if you let something be "good enough"? Say it out loud or write it down.*

CREATIVE FREEDOM

Day 132: The Lie We Learned

Have you ever said, *I don't have a creative bone in my body?* That phrase is harmful because it's not true. It's conditioning that keeps you from even trying. Creativity isn't just painting or music. It shows up in the way you pack a suitcase to make sure everything fits, the way you tell a story that makes your friends laugh, the way you throw a meal together from whatever's in the fridge. When you believe you're not creative, you cut yourself off from play, expression, and new possibilities. You miss the chance to see yourself as resourceful and original. Releasing that belief gives you more freedom and confidence. Everyone is creative, including you.

Me Moment: *Notice if you've ever said or thought I'm not creative. Catch that phrase and rewrite it. Try: I am creative in ways I haven't given myself credit for. Then name one real-life example, no matter how small.*

Day 133: Remembering

You've loosened the grip. You've questioned the rules and taken a closer look at perfectionism. You are creative—innately, naturally, fully. This is a return to what's already within you. You're remembering what never left.

Me Moment: *Look back on the past few days. What surprised you? What felt good? What felt awkward? Did anything change when you stopped needing to be good and started letting it be real?*

Day 134: A Family Affair

Every day, you and your kids are creating together—moments, memories, even the rhythm of your lives. Collaboration is part of family life, and when you loosen control, you open space for flow. Things feel more exciting, more alive. And when you release the need for a perfect outcome, you also model for your kids how to think critically, explore freely, and trust their own ideas instead of simply following along.

Me Moment: *Invite your kids into a round robin exercise. Start a drawing or a story, then take turns adding to it. Let go of control and follow wherever it leads, even if it's silly or unexpected. The goal isn't the finished product—it's the act of creating together.*

Day 135: Five-Minute Flow

You may not have hours of quiet time or the perfect setup. But do you have five minutes? Taking small bits of time to flex your creative muscle—doodle, draw, dance, whatever floats your boat—trains you to create without waiting for perfect conditions. If you can create in the middle of ordinary life, you remind yourself that the simple act of beginning will help you build momentum in everything you do.

Me Moment: *Give yourself five minutes to create today. Jot down a few lines, sketch a shape, hum a tune, or rearrange a corner of your space. Keep it light and playful—growth often begins with the smallest sparks.*

Day 136: Unedit Yourself

Trying to make everything pretty or polished often means you're following someone else's standards instead of letting your own ideas flow. When you edit yourself to fit what looks "right," you cut off the chance to discover your own style, rhythm, and voice. Creativity isn't about the outcome; it's about the process. When you stop editing and let the mess happen, your brain learns it's safe to experiment. And when you experiment, you uncover new ideas and more freedom to express yourself.

Me Moment: *Grab a piece of paper and use your non-dominant hand to draw your childhood home, or any place from memory. Notice what happens when it comes out messy. Do you catch yourself trying to "make it pretty"? Where else in your life might you be stifling flow in order to polish things up or meet someone else's idea of perfect?*

Day 137: Inspired Ritual

If you want life to feel different, it starts with what happens in your mind. New thoughts lead to new choices, and new choices shape your days. Inspiration is what sparks those shifts. If you find it hard to feel inspired, or you're wondering how to start, don't wait for a lightning bolt to strike out of nowhere. Create a small practice that opens the door to possibility. A simple ritual like lighting a candle, opening a notebook, or taking a few breaths becomes a way to invite those sparks forward. What do you think may unfold if you had a daily inspiration ritual?

Me Moment: *Create a small ritual today to invite inspiration. Take a breath, pick up a pen, or open a fresh page. Treat it as an experiment: what possibilities could open if you made this a habit?*

Day 138: Move the Energy

Movement is one of the simplest ways to change how you feel. When you move with intention, you shift your state. Energy gets unstuck, new ideas surface, and emotions have somewhere to go. This is a form of expression just as much as words or art.

Me Moment: *Today, treat movement as an experiment. Move your body—take a walk around the block, dance around the house to your favourite song, or stretch out on the floor. Then notice: Does it lift your mood? Does it spark ideas, make you more playful, or help you see something differently? Pay attention to how movement impacts your capacity to create.*

Day 139: Be Seen

Sharing something you've made can feel scary. It brings up all the old fears: *Will they get it? Will they judge it?* But choosing to share anyway, not for validation but because it matters to you, is a powerful act of self-devotion. It says, *This came from me and that's enough.*

Me Moment: *Pick one small thing you've created and share it with someone you trust. A poem, a playlist, a photo, a sketch, a recipe. You're not asking for feedback; you're honouring your voice. This is you standing behind what you made. That's power.*

CREATIVE FREEDOM

Day 140: You've Been Creative All Along

These past two weeks weren't about turning you into an artist. They were about noticing where your unique, natural expression already lives. It's in the way you make up a silly game to keep your kids entertained, or the way you find a fresh solution when things don't go as planned. This journey was an invitation to recognize that creativity has always been part of you; it just needed space to breathe.

Me Moment: *How has your definition of creativity shifted over these last two weeks? What have you reclaimed? What part of you feels more free, more open, or more real? Write it down or capture it in your own way.*

Day 141
The Rut Report

The next fourteen days aren't about blowing up your life. They're about gently, deliberately interrupting the cycles that have gone flat. The ones that may look fine from the outside but feel dull on the inside. You'll begin to notice what's running on autopilot, not to judge it, but to calibrate and make space for fresh vitality to enter.

Over the next two weeks, you'll play with the art of shaking things up on purpose. Not with big life changes, but with small, unexpected choices that pull you out of default mode and drop you back into active control of yourself. You'll kindle your spark with tiny rebellions—breaking your own rules, skipping the "shoulds," and moving through your day in ways that feel more energizing. You'll be stepping back from what drains you and leaning into what delights you. You get to choose how you move through the world—and it gets to be fun.

Let's shake up the everyday, one playful disruption at a time.

You know that feeling when everything in your day *works*, but nothing quite *wakes* you? That's a rut. Routines can be helpful scaffolding, but when they lose meaning, they start to mute the juiciness of life.

Me Moment: *Today, without changing anything, walk yourself through a "normal" day—from how you wake up to how you wind down. What moments feel dry, dull, or obligatory? What parts feel like you're just going through the motions? Make a short list, then ask, What do I wish felt different here?*

Day 142: Autopilot Awareness

You brush your teeth, scroll your phone, pour your tea—all without really being there. Autopilot sneaks in when your brain decides something is predictable enough to skip over. But presence is where personal power lives. We can't throw glitter on every part of our day, but we can bring more presence to the unconscious moments. This is how you begin to consciously transform the ordinary into something that supports how you truly want to feel.

Me Moment: *Pick one part of your day that usually happens without a second thought, like getting dressed, driving, or prepping lunch. Today, do it with full awareness. Narrate it to yourself if it helps. How does it feel to be there? What details do you usually miss?*

Day 143: The Should Trap

Many of the routines and habits you follow weren't consciously chosen. They're based on "shoulds" you picked up from family, culture, or past versions of yourself. These rules can feel like obligations rather than aligned choices. The practice is to notice one of those routines, question where it came from, and explore how you might approach it differently.

Me Moment: *Pick one part of your routine that feels heavy or automatic. Ask: Where did I get this from? Do I still want it? Imagine how you could shift it so it feels more supportive and true to you.*

Day 144: The Reward Loop

Every routine has a payoff, even uninspiring routines. Maybe you scroll your phone at night because it gives you a hit of dopamine, a moment of simulated connection, or a way to check out. Maybe you avoid shaking things up because predictability feels safer than possibility. There's often a hidden reward beneath the surface of routines.

Me Moment: *Choose one habit or routine that feels stuck. Ask yourself, What am I getting out of this, really? Stimulation? Numbness? Comfort? Control? Then ask, What do I actually want here, and is there a more energizing way to get it? Bringing awareness to your patterns creates space for new possibilities. You get to choose how you meet your needs.*

Day 145: Secret Longings

We're so used to brushing off our longings as unrealistic or frivolous—or worse, feeling guilty for even having them—that we stop hearing them altogether. But those whispers hold wisdom, especially when it comes to shaking up the norm.

Me Moment: *If no one were watching, judging, or expecting you to show up a certain way, what would you change this week . . . just for the joy of it? Would you dress differently? Take yourself out for a nice meal? Say no to something? Make a list of your "If I could, I would . . ." answers. Then circle one to try.*

Day 146: Morning, My Way

Mornings can set the tone for the day or steamroll you into survival mode. Most of us don't consciously design our mornings; we just respond—to the kids, the emails, the clock, the chaos. We move from task to task, trying to keep up, but what if, even just for a moment, your morning became a love letter to your Favourite Self?

Me Moment: *Without aiming for perfection, reimagine your ideal morning vibe. What would it feel like—calm, playful, luxurious, unrushed? What's one small change (music, lighting, clothing, your wake up routine) that could move you a step closer? Try it tomorrow and take note of what shifts.*

Day 147: Pattern Interrupted

You've spent the past few days noticing the grooves you tend to fall into—and are maybe even starting to step out of. Change doesn't always happen in big leaps. Often, it unfolds through intentional slower steps, softer choices, or the decision to do one thing differently.

Me Moment: *Look back on the past six days. Did you disrupt anything? Even in thought? What surprised you? What felt good? What felt hard? This isn't about overhauling your life. It's about building trust that even small or soft shifts can reawaken something in you.*

Day 148: The Tiny Rebellion

When life feels dull or misaligned, the impulse might be to fully uproot or burn it all down—take a new job, move to a new city, create a new version of you—but most of the time, you don't actually need a full reinvention, you just need to breathe new life into what's already there. Sometimes it's the smallest disruptions, the ones no one else even notices, that remind you that you have agency, you get to choose, and your happiness doesn't have to follow the rules.

Me Moment: *If there's a part of your life you've wanted to burn down, pause and ask, What do I actually want instead? Don't concentrate on what you're trying to escape, but what you're craving more of. Name it. Then choose one small way to invite that into your day. True, meaningful, and lasting change takes root by focusing on what you want and building from there.*

Day 149: Remix the Ordinary

There's magic in the mundane if you're willing to play with it. The ordinary isn't the enemy; it's the repetition without reverence that is draining. When you approach your routines like a remix instead of a rerun, they become a canvas for creativity.

Me Moment: *Pick one ordinary habit today—dropping the kids off, getting dressed, doing the dishes—and add some sparkle to it. Put on a playlist you'd usually reserve for a road trip. Do your skincare routine like you're on a vintage perfume ad. Narrate it like a cooking show. Notice what changes in you when the task is given a new script.*

Day 150: Resource Yourself

The everyday tasks—laundry, meal prep, budgeting—can feel endless. But what if they aren't just chores? What if they're a way of resourcing yourself—laying the groundwork for more ease ahead? Every choice you make today is a gift for the you who wakes up tomorrow. A stocked fridge, a cleared inbox, a set of clothes ready for the morning—these simple acts are more than boxes to check. They're love notes forward, small investments that allow your future self to act with more ease and assurance.

Me Moment: *Pick one routine task and do it as a way of resourcing tomorrow's you. When it's done, pause to give thanks—for the care you've given yourself now, and for the ease you've already created for the version of you who's on her way.*

Day 151: Words Matter

Your words paint your world. The words you chose to describe your life carry weight; they hold energy and shape your experience, and they become habits—automatic, familiar, and often unnoticed. Every word carries a frequency. Some feel heavy, others expansive. Some make us feel like we're constantly fixing, chasing, or proving. Others remind us we're already whole.

Me Moment: *Today, you're tuning in to some common word choices when it comes to creating a life you love. Tune in and select the words that feel most uplifting to you and your goals. Is your morning a routine or a ritual? Are you committing to discipline or showing up with devotion? Are you doing the work or walking the journey? Are you healing or integrating? Neither word is fundamentally better than the other. There's no right answer—just insight into what feels true for you right now.*

Day 152: More, Please!

You're allowed to want more, even when things are already good. Wanting more doesn't mean you're ungrateful, it means you're paying attention. When something feels good, you can name it and ask for more of it. That simple act teaches your brain and body that life can keep expanding, and that you are safe to ask for more of what makes you happy. The more you notice and invite it, the more of it you'll experience.

Me Moment: *Today, when you catch yourself in a moment that feels good—a tender exchange with your partner, a shared laugh with your kids, an uplifting chat with a friend, a breathtaking sunset, or even the breeze and birdsong outside—pause. Close your eyes and say, "Yes, more of this, please!"*

Day 153: Just Do It

"I'll let myself enjoy it when . . ." Sound familiar? Most of us have internalized the pattern of delaying joy until the to-do list is complete, the house is clean, the inbox is empty, or we've earned some invisible gold star. But joy isn't a reward; it's a resource. Waiting for the "right" time only reinforces the belief that you're not allowed to feel good right now. You don't need to hustle for permission. You can just give it to yourself.

Me Moment: *Think of one thing you've been holding back from yourself—a rest, a treat, a walk, booking the trip—because you felt you had to earn it first. Now ask: What if I gave myself this simply because filling my own cup doesn't need proof or productivity? Then take one step toward giving it to yourself today.*

Day 154: Zoom Out

When you disrupt the routine, you do more than change what you do—you change how you feel in your own life. Momentum builds not from sweeping changes, but from honouring the small whisper that says, *this could be different*. And then, choosing to do something out of the ordinary.

Me Moment: *Look back on the past two weeks. What did you shake up? What felt more alive, more honest, more you? And what do you want to keep carrying forward? Zoom out and see the throughline; you don't need to escape your life—you just need to keep choosing it.*

Day 155

Your Feeling Tone

Your essence is the way your spirit moves when it's unfiltered and unedited. When you move in alignment with your essence, especially in the small, ordinary moments, you expand your energy, your magnetism, and your reality.

Over these next days, you'll tune in to what feels most like *you*. This category offers more days than the ones before it, an open invitation to linger, to deepen, and to embody your essence more fully.

Beneath your habits, your roles, and even your personality, there's a vibration that is uniquely *you*. Your "feeling tone" is a subtle but powerful frequency that shapes how you move through the world. It's not a mood or emotion; it's the energetic fingerprint of your essence. When you're aligned with it, you feel clear, electric, at ease. When you're not, life starts to feel flat, forced, or foggy.

Me Moment: *Let's tune in. Close your eyes. Take a few slow breaths. Drop your attention beneath your thoughts and into your body. Ask gently, What is my unique feeling tone? Not a word, not a colour, just a sensation. A quality of being that's unmistakably you. Notice how it shows up; maybe as warmth, stillness, a subtle pulse, or a deep ease. Then ask: What pulls me out of this feeling? What helps me return to it? Write down what arises. This is how you begin to recognize the signal of your essential self.*

Day 156: The Most You

You may not have known it at the time, but in those moments when you felt vibrant, alive, or totally in flow, you were tuned in to your *feeling tone*. You weren't overthinking or performing. You were *being*. That's the version of you we're calling forward now.

Me Moment: *Reflect on three to five moments from your life when you felt lit up, deeply present, or effortlessly yourself. What were you doing? Who were you with (or were you alone)? How did it feel in your body? Chances are that your feeling tone was leading the way. Write down your observations and what you want more of.*

Day 157: Essence Versus Identity

Your essence is who you *are*. Your identity is who you've learned to *be*. One is fluid, intuitive, and self-sourced. The other is shaped by expectations, past roles, and social conditioning. It's not that identity is bad—it just sometimes drowns out the signal of your deeper self.

Me Moment: *Make two quick lists in two columns. On the first column write "Learned Identity" and add in words or roles you've picked up over time (e.g., responsible, overachiever, helper, peacemaker). On the second column, write "True Essence" and add in words that feel like your inner compass (e.g., radiant, wild, thoughtful, funny, sensual). Then compare the two lists. Where do they feel different? Where are you living more from learned identity than essence—and where might you be ready to let your essence lead?*

Day 158: The Perfect Mum

Motherhood has a way of rewriting your identity. In the chaos of becoming everything for a new, little someone, parts of you can get buried—not because they stopped mattering, but because they got covered by a thousand silent expectations and the pressure to live up to some illusive standard. Over time, this pressure can overshadow your actual truth.

Me Moment: *What have you been led to believe "good moms" should be like? List three to five unspoken rules you've picked up (e.g., moms don't take time for themselves, moms are always grateful, moms don't dress like that). Then ask yourself these questions: Which of these are mine? Which ones am I ready to release so I can show up as my whole self again?*

Day 159: What She Knows

Self-perception shapes everything—how you move through the world, what you believe you deserve, and how much space you allow yourself to take up. When you've spent years adjusting to roles and expectations, it's only natural to lose touch with your true essence. But your Favourite Self is still in there. The version of you who remembers what really matters and who you really are is waiting to share her wisdom.

Me Moment: *Close your eyes and feel into your Favourite Self. She's steady, grounded, and fully you. What does she want to remind you of today? Write it as a message from her to you. Keep it close. Return to it any time the old rules creep back in.*

Day 160: Embodied Clues

Your body knows when you're in alignment and when you're out of sync. It speaks in sensations: expansion or tightness, spark or drain. When you're rooted in your essence, you feel it. There's ease in your breath, clarity in your movement, and a quiet kind of power in your presence.

Me Moment: *Close your eyes and scan your body as you call your Favourite Self to the surface. Ask her to fill your body with her energy. What does that feel like—posture, breath, voice, presence? Now think of a time when you were out of alignment—what did that feel like? These physical clues are your compass. Start paying attention to what your body is telling you when you walk into a room, make a choice, and stand firm in your truth.*

Day 161: Essence Rising

You've been peeling back layers, tuning in to your feeling tone, and reclaiming what's always been yours. A version of you that feels more honest, more alive, more *you* is finding its way to the surface. That's your essence rising.

Me Moment: *What parts of you have started to come back online this week? Is there a new way you're thinking or speaking about yourself? Something new you're noticing about yourself? Maybe a new way you're dressing? Jot down three shifts, small or big, that signal you're in greater alignment. Then ask, What does my essence want more of this week?*

Day 162: Dress the Part

A really fun way to stay in conversation with your essence is through small, sensory rituals—ones that don't need to be seen by anyone else. Things as simple as a fancy pair of underwear, a luxurious body oil, a bracelet worn just for you, or something else that gives you pleasure. These quiet choices send a clear signal: *I'm the sparkle under the surface.*

Me Moment: *Choose something to wear, apply, or carry today that feels like a private nod to your Favourite Self. Make it a special secret, intentional and connected: a scent, a texture, a layer no one else knows about. Let it shift the way you move, even if only you can feel it.*

Day 163: Speak from the Source

When you speak from your essence, something shifts. Your words land with clarity, not performance. Your voice becomes less about proving and more about *presence*. Whether you're setting a boundary, telling the truth, or simply expressing a need, your life force leads the way.

Me Moment: *Today, choose one moment to practice speaking from your centre. It might be saying what you actually want for dinner. Or finally expressing something you've been holding back. Pause first, drop into your body, then speak—not from pressure or politeness, but from your inner knowing. See what happens when your voice and your truth align.*

INNER FLAME

Day 164: Radiate, Don't Rescue

When you start stepping more fully into your true essence, one that is more joyful and lighter, it's natural to want to bring others with you. You might even start to measure your growth by how well it lands and how much it shifts the energy around you. And when others don't meet you there, it can feel jarring, even discouraging. There's often a pull to coach, teach, or preach what you've learned. But your journey is *yours*. You don't have to translate your transformation for anyone else. Your joy doesn't need to be justified, proven, or shared to be real.

Me Moment: *Today, do something that lights you up without thinking about how it's received; jump on the bed, wear the bright scarf, tell the joke, and then let it be. Notice how it feels to hold your energy without shrinking it or offering it as proof of worth.*

Day 165: Your Main Ingredients

Your essence is made up of a one-of-a-kind blend—your own mix of traits, quirks, moods, and gifts. Some parts of you are sweet, some bring the heat, some are complex and hard to pin down, but every ingredient matters. It's the full mix that makes you . . . you. When you stop trying to water yourself down and start honouring your whole recipe, life gets richer, more aligned, and more alive.

Me Moment: *Imagine you had to hand the recipe that makes you up to someone else—someone who wanted to care for you well. What would your instructions say? Write down three to five qualities that make up your essence and then add a few directions for helping you thrive. Think along the lines of: "Needs sunlight," "Let her take her time," "Don't interrupt her dreaming," or "Add movement daily."*

Day 166: One Step Up

You don't have to jump from fear to bliss in one move. The most powerful shifts often come from choosing just one better-feeling thought. Frustration can soften into hope. Discouragement can lighten into relief. Remember: you are the sky; emotions are the weather moving through. Each small shift clears a little more space for your light to shine.

Me Moment: *As you move through your day, notice when heavier emotions like frustration, anger, fear or resentment show up. Pause and ask: Is this how I want to feel? What would bring even a small sense of relief right now? Each gentle shift is proof that the weather can change, while you remain steady.*

Day 167: Magnetic in Motion

When you see your vision not as a far-off fantasy, but as something that already belongs to you, that's already unfolding from your heart and your efforts, your energy starts organising around it. Your brain doesn't know the difference between imagination and memory, it just follows your lead. So, when you begin treating your desires like part of your normal, everyday life, they stop feeling like a reach and start becoming real.

Me Moment: *Pick one dream you've been holding—something that feels big, exciting, maybe even out of reach. Now ask: If this were already true, how would I move through today? What would I think about? What would I no longer waste energy on? Because one day soon, it will be your new normal.*

Day 168: Amplify You

Over the past few weeks, you've remembered how it feels to move from your centre, speak from your truth, and live in a way that amplifies what's already within you. That's your signature frequency—undeniably yours, unmistakably radiant.

Me Moment: *Reflect on the past few weeks. What's felt most like you lately. What thoughts, choices, or rituals brought your Favourite Self forward? What felt natural, easeful, or quietly powerful? Write down one way your essence showed up—and choose one you want to keep amplifying.*

Day 169: Main Character Energy

Imagine your life as a movie. You're sitting in the audience, watching yourself. What would you be rooting for her to do? Deep down, you already know what's calling you. You feel it deep in your bones and in your heart, pulsing in the back of your mind. When you name what you truly want, and take even the tiniest step toward it, you build self-trust. You stop waiting for the perfect moment and start becoming the person who moves, even with shaky hands.

Me Moment: *Ask yourself: If I were rooting for me, what would I want myself to do next? Then invite yourself to take one small, inspired action toward that dream. Nothing more, nothing less.*

Day 170: Micro-Adventure

A micro-adventure is anything that breaks your routine in the name of your spark. It doesn't have to be big. It just has to feel a little spontaneous, a little unnecessary, a little fun. You don't need a plan. You just need a *yes*.

Me Moment: *Say yes to one small adventure today. Take the scenic route. Try the coffee shop you've never been to. Wander a bookstore with no goal. Dance while you fold laundry. Keep it light, playful, and just for you. Then ask yourself, What shifted in me because I said yes to that?*

Day 171: Playlist Reboot

Back on Day 26, you created a playlist to reflect your Favourite Self—a soundscape for how you wanted to feel, express yourself, and come alive. Now that you've come this far, you may notice that version of your Favourite Self has stretched, softened, deepened, or surprised you. That's what this work is meant to do. You are not meant to stay fixed; you're meant to grow.Imagine this playlist as a dynamic symbol of your evolution—something that shifts with you.

Me Moment: *Revisit the playlist you created. Notice what still resonates and what you're ready to release. Add a few new songs that feel aligned with who you are now. This simple edit is more than music; it's a celebration of your unfolding. And if you never created one, that's okay! Now's your chance to give your evolution a soundtrack.*

Day 172: So Extra

There's a version of you who loves a little drama, flair, or sparkle—not for attention, but for expression. Being "extra" isn't about proving anything. It's about honouring the bigness of your essence—whether that shows up in how you speak, how you move, how you lead, and yes, even what you wear. This is about showing up with full colour, full flavour, full you.

Me Moment: *Find one way to be a little extra today; say the thing with more flair, take the long way home with your favourite song blasting, add a dramatic flourish to your storytelling, say yes to something that feels a little too fun for a weekday. Whatever you choose, do it like your Favourite Self is right there with you, cheering you on and daring you to go bigger.*

Day 173: Who Does She Think She Is?

When you start living out loud, someone's going to have thoughts. Maybe even you. That inner voice might whisper, *Who does she think she is?* And the answer is: someone who's done hiding, someone who's finally showing up as herself.

Me Moment: *Make a list of the things you worry people might think if you fully lived as your Favourite Self. Then write a response to each one—not to defend yourself, but to own it.*

Day 174: Just Choose

You don't need a bulletproof reason to want what you want—desire is enough. Today is about choosing without overjustifying, overthinking, or overexplaining—even to yourself. Sovereign and simple is the secret sauce today.

Me Moment: *Make one choice today, small or big, just because it feels right for you. Not because it's practical. Not because it makes sense. Not because someone else would approve. Just because it's what you want. Then notice how freeing that was.*

Day 175: Pull Up Another Chair

Empowered women empower others. The moment you reclaim your spark, your voice, your seat at the table you create a ripple. One of the most joyful things you can do with your power is to pass it on. Pull up another chair. Share the mic. Make someone else feel seen. Lifting another woman doesn't take anything from you—it multiplies the magic.

 Me Moment: *Think of a woman who brings light to your world—or someone who might need a little of yours right now. Reach out. Send a voice note, a text, or a message that reminds her of who she is. Uplifting others is one of the fastest ways to remember your own radiance.*

INNER FLAME

Day 176: Celebration Station

Celebration isn't just for milestones, it's a way of honouring the *you* that's here now. When you pause to recognize yourself, you start to build a life that feels good as it's happening, not just when goals are met. The way you've been showing up—reflecting, experimenting, expressing—it deserves to be celebrated. Especially by you.

Me Moment: *Create a five-minute self-celebration ritual, just because. Light a candle. Put on a song that makes you feel like you. Look in the mirror and say three things you love or appreciate about yourself right now, as you are.*

Day 177: Brag Practice

Bragging gets a bad rap, but owning your brilliance is a radical act of self-respect. When you share what you're proud of, you're not only normalizing your success, but also creating room for more. You're not asking for validation. You're stating a truth; you've grown, you're glowing, and you know it.

Me Moment: *Write down five things you're proud of right now—tiny wins, big shifts, moments you showed up. Then share one; say it out loud, text it to a friend, post it to social media if you want to. This isn't arrogance. It's ownership.*

Day 178: Joy Break

Joy doesn't need to be earned. It's a powerful choice. The more often you choose it, the more natural it becomes to access it—not as a reward, but as your right.

Me Moment: *Take a joy break today. Five minutes. That's it. Step outside and feel the sun. Put your phone down and stretch. Skip to your car. Dance to a song. Toss compliments like confetti. Whatever reminds you that joy is available to you right now—do that.*

Day 179: All the Way Alive

You're here to feel your life—awake to beauty, sensation, meaning, and emotion. That's the pulse behind everything we've practiced—presence, boldness, pleasure, play. Being fully tuned in is a choice you keep making: a decision to show up, feel deeply, and live in colour.

Me Moment: *Write yourself a reminder that pulls you back to what matters. Something like, Tending to my spark is a non-negotiable. Place it somewhere visible—mirror, dashboard, or lock screen. Each time you see it, reconnect with yourself.*

Day 180: Midway Milestone!

You've been walking this journey for half a year. That's 180 days of tuning in, experimenting, remembering, and becoming. It's easy to gloss over milestones, but this is worth pausing for.

Me Moment: *Write yourself a note of acknowledgement—simple and honest: I'm proud of how I've shown up. Take a breath and recognize this version of you standing here. Then keep going, with that truth in your back pocket.*

Phase Three: Own the Room

Phase Three is where you'll stop caring about approval and start caring more about living authentically.

You'll start with Days 181 to 194, where you'll begin to notice the small ways you might still dim your light—deflecting compliments, hiding quirks, questioning your shine—and begin practicing what it feels like to let yourself be seen.

Next, we'll move into Days 195 to 208, where you'll explore boundaries and authenticity. You'll stop shape-shifting for approval, learn to honour your yeses and nos, and discover what it's like to connect without self-abandonment.

From there, Days 209 to 222 take you into perfectionism's grip and out the other side. You'll trade constant striving for presence, explore the difference between excellence and proving, and begin creating from a place of enoughness.

In Days 223 to 236, you'll practice bold embodiment. Through movement, voice, and presence, you'll take up space on your terms.

Building on that foundation, Days 237 to 250 invite you to tune in to your natural rhythm. You'll explore how cycles, seasons, and personal pace can guide your choices and help you release urgency in favour of alignment.

Finally, Days 251 to 264 bring this phase to a close with celebration. You'll learn to recognize progress, honour your brilliance, and shift from critique to appreciation—of yourself, your relationships, and your journey so far.

This phase is where things start to click. One choice at a time, you'll see what it feels like to stop hiding and fully own the room.

Day 181

Where Do You Dim?

So many of us have inherited the belief that being fully ourselves—bold, expressive, unapologetic—will cost us love or belonging. That if we shine too brightly, we'll somehow push people away. That being fully yourself is risky. You don't always notice it when it happens: a small pullback, a lowered voice, a compliment dodged with a joke. Shrinking becomes so habitual that it's second nature.

Visibility isn't just about being visible to others. It's about letting the parts you once kept hidden—your joy, your success, your power, your weirdness, your depth—come up for air without apology. Because owning the room isn't about being loud. It's about being real.

This section is about gently unraveling those stories. You'll notice where you hold back, where you second-guess, where you've downplayed your own radiance. Then you'll take small steps to let more of yourself be seen—not just the parts you've already made peace with, but the parts that still feel big, or are a little wild, or a little intimidating.

Me Moment: *At the end of the day, name one moment where you noticed yourself shrinking. Say, "I see you," and imagine gently turning up the light instead.*

Day 182: The Safety of Small

Over time, you may have picked up the idea that being in your power—successful, happy, attractive, wealthy—puts you at risk of judgement, rejection, and isolation. So, you start to pull back, just a little. Tone down a dream, downplay a win, keep the joy quiet. Not because you don't want more, but because being fully seen feels . . . complicated. But hiding your light doesn't protect you. It disconnects you from yourself. Today, it's time to shine a light on the fears lurking beneath the surface.

Me Moment: *Fill in the blanks: If I'm too _________, then people will _________. Let yourself answer it a few times. Then ask yourself: Where did that belief come from? Is it even mine? No need to fix it, just meet it with honesty and compassion.*

Day 183: Stand In It

Your body tells the truth before your mind catches up. In moments of visibility, your posture, breath, and subtle tension reveal what you really believe about being seen. Dimming your light doesn't always mean making yourself small. It can look like over-smiling, over-explaining, or holding yourself rigid. These patterns are responses your body learned to feel safe, but over time, they also keep you from feeling fully expressed.

Me Moment: *Today, simply notice how your body responds when you're being witnessed. For a breath or two, let your Favourite Self's posture and poise lead the way.*

Day 184: The Art of Receiving

Brushing off a compliment isn't humility, it's self-rejection dressed up as politeness. Maybe you were taught that deflecting praise was graceful, modest, even admirable. But it's not. It's a quiet insult to your own brilliance. When you can't receive something as simple as kind words, that resistance doesn't stay small—it spills into everything. Your ability to receive joy, love, support, or opportunity is a skill, a practice. A yes to your own enoughness.

Me Moment: *Next time someone compliments you, pause, breathe, and let it land. Just say thank you, and feel the shift of letting it in.*

Day 185: Let Them See You

One of the most powerful gifts you can give your children is letting them see *you*—not just the mum who gets things done, but the woman who laughs, creates, rests, dreams, and owns her worth. Kids learn more from what we model than what we say. When you allow yourself to be fully expressed, you show them what it looks like to belong to yourself.

Me Moment: *Today, intentionally let your kids witness a moment of you being fully you, whether it's expressing an opinion, enjoying a hobby, or celebrating yourself. Let them see what self-worth looks like in action.*

Day 186: Power Stance

Research shows that standing tall, opening your chest, and grounding your stance can reduce stress and boost confidence. The way you hold yourself sends signals to your brain: *I am safe. I belong.* Visibility starts in the body, long before words are spoken.

Me Moment: *Notice how you hold your body as you move through the day. Practice softening your shoulders, lifting through your heart, and grounding through your feet. Spend a few minutes in front of a mirror, exploring how your Favourite Self stands, breathes, and holds space.*

Day 187: Noticing the Shift

Take a moment to notice how far you've come, even in small ways. Maybe you're catching yourself in the act of dimming. Maybe you're softening your posture when being witnessed. Maybe you've realized how often you shrink out of habit. Every ounce of awareness you bring to your inner landscape—the good stuff and the sticky parts—matters!

Me Moment: *Write about one moment this week where you felt more present, more open, or more unapologetically yourself. Name it. Celebrate it.*

Day 188: Inherently Beautiful

You become radiant when you stop being at war with what is naturally yours. The curl that refuses to lie flat, the nose that carries your lineage, a birthmark that tells a story—these are not things to tame or fix, they're the very traits that make you unforgettable. True beauty can't be found chasing a standard someone else made up. It's the radiance that happens when you finally start accepting, enhancing, and owning what's truly yours.

Me Moment: *Stand in front of the mirror and choose one feature you've resisted or tried to hide. Instead of correcting it, honour it. Name it as part of your beauty. Ask: What if this has always been one of my most beautiful traits?*

Day 189: Not Your Standards

The way you see beauty has been shaped over time by the images, messages, and unspoken expectations that surround you. Many of those standards were never meant to help you feel at home in your own skin; they were meant to keep you questioning yourself. Beauty standards shift constantly. What's rejected in one era is worshipped in another. When you notice this, you begin to see how fragile those rules really are.

Me Moment: *Make a quick list of the beauty standards you've absorbed over the years—what you were told was "in" or "ideal." Then look at your list and remind yourself: these are not truths, they're trends. Cross them out. Now, name one feature or quality that has always been yours, no matter what the world says is "in." That's the kind of beauty you can trust.*

Day 190: Work It

There's power in claiming your favourite features and highlighting them, not to impress others but to delight yourself. A bold colour on full lips, a haircut that lets your natural texture live free, a necklace that frames your collarbone. Enhancing what you love is an act of reverence.

Me Moment: *Write down one physical trait you love about yourself. Now think: How could you enhance it today in a way that feels reverent? Then do it. Not for the gaze of others, but for your own celebration.*

Day 191: The Invention of Flaws

Did you know the word "cellulite" didn't exist in common language until an article in a high-fashion magazine introduced it in the 1960s? The magazine framed it as a new "condition" and then advertised cures. Many so-called flaws were invented as a way to sell products. The truth: they were never flaws at all.

Me Moment: *Think of one "flaw" you've battled with. Research when and how society began labeling it as such. Then ask yourself: If no one had ever told me this was wrong, how would I feel about it?*

Day 192: Beauty as Presence

Beauty goes far beyond physical features. It lives in the way you carry yourself—ease instead of tension, confidence instead of comparison, a solid connection to who you are. It's the light in your eyes when you laugh, the way your face softens when you're at peace, the warmth you bring into a room. Presence is what people remember, and your beauty expands when you let yourself be fully seen.

Me Moment: Today, practice activating beauty as presence. Slow your pace, soften your shoulders, and connect to your breath. Carry yourself as if you already know you are beautiful. Then notice: Where do you see beauty reflected back—through someone's smile, a kind glance, or even the colors around you? Beauty grows when you live inside it.

Day 193: A Beautiful Life

You can create beauty just as much as you can exude it. The way you dress a table, arrange flowers, choose colors, or style your hair is all an extension of you. When you intentionally create beauty around you, it echoes back and reminds you of the beauty within.

Me Moment: Today, create one small thing of beauty. It could be the way you plate your lunch, the arrangement of books on your desk, or a simple braid in your hair. Make it for you and notice how the act of creating beauty awakens it in you.

Day 194: Radiantly You

In the previous days, you've explored beauty as something deeper than standards or trends. You've noticed what's always been yours, examined the messages that shaped you, reclaimed what was never a flaw, and practiced beauty as presence.

Me Moment: *Reflect on what shifted for you these last several days. What did you learn about your unique beauty? What messages or old stories are you ready to release? How can you keep honouring the beauty that is yours, today and every day?*

Day 195
Shape-Shifting

The more you understand your own energy, the more naturally you'll draw in relationships that feel nourishing, easy, and real. When you trust yourself, you stop shape-shifting and start connecting. You speak with more clarity. You listen with more presence. You stop abandoning yourself in the name of keeping the peace.

Here, you'll explore what it means to stay rooted in your truth while showing up fully for the people you love. You'll practice honouring your needs without guilt, voicing your yes and your no with confidence, and making space for the kind of connection that lets everyone exhale.

When you feel at home in yourself, your relationships can finally feel like home too.

Without realizing it, many of us fall into the habit of adjusting ourselves to fit in. Maybe it's softening your opinions, over-explaining, or ignoring your own needs to keep the peace. This shape-shifting can feel like connection, but it often comes at the expense of your authenticity. Today is about gently noticing where that shows up.

Me Moment: *As you move through your day, pay attention to moments when you tweak or filter yourself to fit in. Ask yourself quietly: Is this who I want to be right now?*

Day 196: The Safety of Small

People-pleasing can disguise itself as kindness, but it's often rooted in fear—fear of disappointing, fear of conflict, fear of being less likeable. But true connection isn't built on self-abandonment. When you say yes to others at the expense of yourself, you disconnect from your own truth, so they're no longer connecting with the real you. Boundaries aren't walls; they're bridges to more honest relationships.

Me Moment: *Today, notice when you feel the pull to say "yes" or "no" out of obligation, not truth, then pause and consider a different response. Even if you don't change your answer yet, simply notice: What would a truthful answer sound like?*

Day 197: The Boundary of Space

You don't have to explain, entertain, or be available all the time. Some of your most powerful boundaries won't be about saying no to others—but about saying yes to the space you need. When you protect your mental, emotional, and energetic space, you make room for your clarity and creativity to lead. Let the world adjust to the space you're reclaiming.

Me Moment: *Today, choose one area where you can create more energetic space. Maybe it's not replying right away. Maybe it's stepping back before committing. Let that space be a boundary— not a gap to fill.*

Day 198: Relationship Recalibration

In some way or another, we all internalize certain beliefs about what it takes to "belong" in specific social circles, parts of society, or even family. For many of us, that meant being easygoing, agreeable, or selfless. These beliefs often get passed down—through family dynamics, school, and friendships, but belonging built on self-sacrifice isn't true connection; it's a transaction. Real connection allows you to bring your full self to the table.

Me Moment: *Reflect on this: What do I believe is required of me to form a connection? Write down any patterns or phrases that surface. Then ask yourself: Do these beliefs still feel true for the kind of relationships I want now?*

Day 199: The Illusion of Control

Control doesn't always show up as intensity or force. Sometimes it's soft, subtle—disguised as being agreeable, overly accommodating, keeping the peace, or offering kindness you don't feel. That version of "niceness" can be control—a way to manage how others see you, avoid conflict, or influence outcomes. But control tightens; it diminishes your capacity and magnetism. Trust creates space. It softens the nervous system. It reminds you that you don't have to hold it all.

Me Moment: *Notice one moment today where you're managing a reaction, protecting an image, or steering an outcome. Even if it's small, pause, check in with your body—your breath, shoulders, tone—and ask yourself: What would it feel like to stop trying to manage this?*

Day 200: No Big Deal

Setting a boundary does not have to be a big or dramatic moment. It can be a simple, everyday act of honesty—like saying no, asking for space, or expressing a true preference. Practicing these small responses builds self-trust and helps others trust you too.

Me Moment: *Today, notice one opportunity in daily life to say what you really mean or need, in a clear, easy way, without overexplaining or making a big deal out of it.*

Day 201: Coming Home to Yourself

Every time you pause before shape-shifting, every time you notice your impulse to please, you're building a new kind of relationship with yourself. Boundaries aren't harsh lines, instead they're a way of coming home to what feels true for you. They allow you to stay connected to yourself, even while being connected with others. That's real intimacy.

Me Moment: *Write about a moment this week where you felt most aligned with your truth in a relationship. Keep that awareness close as you move forward.*

Day 202: Naming Your Needs

You thrive when your real needs are met—things like space, movement, connection, or time alone. But those needs can get buried under routines, expectations, or the habit of saying yes too quickly. Getting clear on what supports you is the first step. Then comes creating the structure that helps those needs get met.

Me Moment: *Make a quick list of what you need more of to feel like yourself—think solo time, creative space, rest, movement, laughter. Now choose one and ask: What's one simple shift I can make to protect that need? (For example: eating lunch alone instead of joining the group.)*

Day 203: Boundaries Begin with You

The first person you need to set boundaries with is yourself. Not in a rigid, rule-driven way, but in a way that honours your time, energy, and capacity. When you constantly override your own needs for the sake of others (or your to-do list), you erode self-trust. Keeping small promises to yourself builds that trust back.

Me Moment: *Today, choose one small way to honour yourself. Maybe it's finishing work when you said you would. Maybe it's giving yourself the break you promised. Follow through—not for discipline, but for self-respect.*

Day 204: Protect Your Peace

Not every comment, request, or expectation deserves your time and attention. Boundaries include choices about where you place your attention, what you engage with, and what you no longer make available. Protecting your peace can be as simple as not taking the bait, choosing silence over your usual reaction, or mentally stepping back from what's not yours to carry.

Me Moment: *Today, practice protecting your peace. When something tugs at your energy, pause and ask: Do I really want to engage with this? Let yourself choose stillness, without guilt.*

Day 205: Feel Your Yes and No

Your body often knows the truth before your mind catches up. A genuine yes or no feels honest, open, energizing. A yes or no that comes from obligation or people-pleasing feels heavy, constricted, draining. The more you tune into these signals, the easier it becomes to honour them. Boundaries aren't just fixed rules; they're also moment-by-moment check-ins with your body's wisdom. Sometimes they defy logic or explanation. Your yes and your no are reason enough—because your intuition, your boundaries, and your desires don't need justification to be valid.

Me Moment: *Today, practice noticing how your body responds to invitations, requests, or even thoughts. Does your chest expand or tighten? Do you feel pulled forward or resistant? Let these sensations guide your yes and no.*

Day 206: Stay with Yourself

Without even noticing it, you can sometimes lose yourself in conversations—mirroring others, managing their emotions, adjusting your energy to make sure things flow smoothly. But true connection and, ultimately, satisfaction happens when you stay rooted in yourself while relating to others. Presence is a boundary. It keeps you connected to your own truth, even while being engaged and open.

Me Moment: *Today, before you automatically agree, nod along, or soften your truth to keep the peace, pause and ask yourself: Is this really me? This isn't about being argumentative. You can stay lighthearted and connected while staying true to yourself.*

Day 207: Honour the Yes

Saying no gets a lot of attention. But honouring your yes is just as important and often just as hard. It can feel vulnerable to admit what you want, to accept help, or to say yes to opportunities that stretch you. But every time you honour an authentic yes, you strengthen your connection to yourself. You are saying, *I trust my inner knowing. I trust my readiness.*

Me Moment: *Today, when you feel a genuine yes, whether it's to rest, an invitation, or something else exciting, say yes with your whole self, and trust that honouring what feels true is enough.*

Day 208: Authentic Connection

The real gift of honouring your boundaries—your yes, your no, your truth—is that it brings you closer to others, not further away. When you start relating from your whole, honest self, your relationships deepen. You're no longer performing. You're simply showing up as you really are. That's where authentic connection lives.

Me Moment: *Write about a relationship or interaction that has felt easier, lighter, or more honest since you started practicing these shifts. Celebrate that progress. Let it remind you that being true to yourself is always worth it.*

Day 209

The Sneaky Shape of Perfectionism

Perfectionism slips in quietly—just one more tweak, one more draft, one more delay until things feel "ready." It whispers that if you can just get it right, you'll be safe from judgement or failure. You were never meant to live in a constant state of fixing yourself. Your worth isn't hiding in the next goal, the next tweak, the next version of you that's more polished. Perfectionism pulls you into striving; presence brings you back home.

In the next few weeks, you'll practice shifting from performing to expressing, from proving to playing. You'll explore what it feels like to support yourself with care, rather than constantly trying to improve yourself into worthiness.

Perfection keeps you waiting. Life happens when you show up as you are.

Me Moment: *Today, gently notice where perfectionism shows up as over-preparing or over-editing. Catch it with kindness. Ask: Am I refining for clarity—or stalling out of fear?*

Day 210: What's Your Flavour?

Perfectionism wears many masks. For some, it's people-pleasing. For others, it's overachieving, over committing, or avoiding things they're not instantly good at. In motherhood, it might show up as trying to do everything "right" while silently judging yourself for falling short. Your version might be subtle, but it shapes how you move through the world.

Me Moment: *Today, get curious. How does perfectionism show up for you? Is it constant doing? Comparison? Reluctance to ask for help? Name your personal flavor, not to judge, but to gain clarity. If the answers don't come to you right away, that's okay. Just be on the lookout over the next several days and notice with curiosity.*

Day 211: Simply Because You Exist

It's tempting to tie your worth to how much you accomplish, how perfectly you show up, or how well you manage it all. Productivity, success, even being the "good mum" can become stand-ins for self-worth. But you are not your output. You're worthy simply because you exist.

Me Moment: *Today, notice when your inner dialogue tries to measure your value by how much you've done (or how perfectly you've done it). Pause. Remind yourself: I am worthy, even when I'm simply being.*

Day 212: Who Taught You "Perfect?"

Your version of "perfect" didn't appear out of nowhere. It was shaped by family expectations, school, culture, maybe even your own coping strategies. Often, these standards are inherited, not chosen. The good news? You get to decide which ones still belong to you.

Me Moment: *Reflect on this: Where did my beliefs about doing things "the right way" come from? Think of a specific person, place, or experience that shaped your idea of what it means to be "good enough." Are those standards still serving you? This isn't about blaming or pointing fingers, but rather understanding where you learned it and releasing it.*

Day 213: What's at the Root?

Loving beauty, excellence, or having high standards isn't the same as perfectionism. One is rooted in joy, creativity, and alignment. The other is rooted in fear, control, and not-enoughness. The key difference is that high standards inspire and expand you while perfectionism creates pressure and makes it hard to move forward. You're allowed to want things to be beautiful, intentional, and well-crafted. That desire can be sacred, maybe even a super power. The invitation is to notice: *Does this feel expansive or suffocating?*

Me Moment: *Today, reflect on a current project, task, or role. Is your desire for excellence coming from inspiration or fear? Name it, without judgement. Let this clarity guide your next step.*

Day 214: The Pursuit of Perfect

Perfectionism often promises safety: protection from criticism, mistakes, or failure. But there's a hidden cost. Constantly striving to get it "right" can drain your creativity, dim your light, and keep you from meaningful connection. The pursuit of perfect can become so loud, it drowns out the simple pleasure of *being*.

Me Moment: *Ask yourself: What is perfectionism costing me right now? Is it your time, your peace, your relationships with your children? Call it out with compassion and choose where your focus goes next.*

Day 215: Release and Reclaim

You've been untangling the sneaky ways perfectionism shapes your choices—how it seeps into your work, your relationships, even your self-talk. When you let go of the pressure to be perfect, you create space to reclaim what matters.

Me Moment: *Take a moment to explore the following: What am I ready to release when it comes to perfectionism? And just as important: What am I ready to claim in its place? Write both answers down as a loving promise to yourself.*

Day 216: The Play Portal

Studies show that when you shift from performance to play, your brain releases dopamine, lowers stress, and opens creative pathways. But what does that *actually* mean? It means doing something *just* because it feels good. It means loosening your grip on outcomes and letting wonder lead, even if it gets a little messy. Play isn't a reward for finishing your to-do list; it's a way back to yourself. When you stop trying to "get it right," you create space for real flow.

Me Moment: *Today, choose one small task or moment, something low-stakes, and give yourself full permission to let it be fun, not perfect.*

Day 217: Your Excellency

Perfection is rooted in proving, whereas excellence springs from alignment. When your actions feel true to you—when how you show up reflects your values, your light, and your integrity—that's excellence. It's not louder. It's not shinier. It simply fits. The chase for approval is exhausting. But when you pivot from proving to expressing, everything softens. You're no longer performing. You're creating from a place that feels right in your bones.

Me Moment: *Today, reflect on an area where you've been chasing someone else's version of success. Once you've given it some thought, pause and ask yourself: What would excellence look and feel like to you? Write it down. Let that be your guide.*

Day 218: Be Seen Trying

There's a special kind of courage in letting yourself be seen mid-process—before everything is polished, before you have the perfect words, before it all makes sense. When your kids see you trying, they learn it's safe to try too. They learn that figuring it out as you go is not a flaw, it's part of being alive, creative, and brave.

Me Moment: *Today, share something that's still unfolding: a new skill, a project, a messy moment. Let your kids witness you in motion, not to prove anything, but to model what it looks like to stay open, real, and in process.*

Day 219: Good Enough

There's power in deciding something is done. Not when it's perfect, not when it's polished, when it's done. That moment when you choose to release it—not because it's flawless, but because it's good enough. Perfectionism will keep you circling forever. Completion sets you free.

Me Moment: *Today, pick one small thing—a task, a project, a decision—and finish it at "good enough." Then stop. No spiraling. No tweaking. Let it be enough and move on.*

Day 220: Cut the Self-Improvement Strings

The self-help cycle can be sneaky. One more book, one more ritual, one more hack—and suddenly growth becomes a race to stay "on track." But chasing constant upgrades doesn't make you more whole, it makes you more exhausted. Real growth unfolds naturally when you stop measuring yourself against an endless finish line.

Me Moment: *Notice where you've been optimizing—reading, tracking, striving—and set it down for today. Ask yourself: How can I enjoy myself as I am, right now?*

Day 221: Support, Not Self-Improvement

Support is rooted in trust. It says: *I believe in who I am now and I'm here to nurture, aid, and care for that person.* Improvement, when tangled with perfectionism, says, *You're not good enough yet.* One feels like coming home. The other keeps you chasing.

Me Moment: *Today, when you think about your daily goals or big dreams, ask yourself: Am I approaching this to support my growth— or to fix myself?*

Day 222: Being You

Every time you choose to show up as you are—in process, fully human— you reclaim your spark for life. Freedom is found in trusting that you're already enough, right here, right now.

Me Moment: *Write a few lines about a way you've softened perfectionism's grip in your life. Celebrate that shift. Carry that insight into your next step.*

Day 223

Beyond Nice

Being "nice" sounds harmless, but how often has it meant being agreeable at your own expense? So many of us have been praised for being easy, low-maintenance, and accommodating. Bit by bit, that niceness became a habit of self-editing. But there's a difference between being kind and being palatable. Your fullness—your complexity, your boldness—is where real connection lives.

Boldness isn't about volume; it's about alignment. When you show up as your full self—without shrinking, shape-shifting, or softening your edges—you're embodying boldness. There's nothing to prove. Your essence does not require explanation.

In the next few weeks, you'll practice claiming your desires, taking up space, and living in your fullness on purpose. You've explored what it means to be seen—not as a performance, but as an act of self-trust, and in doing so, you've become a permission slip for everyone around you to do the same.

Me Moment: *Today, fill in this blank: I'd rather be called _________ than "nice." Which word did you choose? Complicated? Direct? Passionate? Something else? Explore and honour your depth and nuance.*

Day 224: The Fear of Outgrowing

One of the sneakiest fears that can keep people from rising to their full potential is the fear of outgrowing your people. You worry: *If I grow, if I take up more space, if I step into my power . . . will they come with me?* Sometimes, we stay small to keep old dynamics comfortable. But silencing your spark isn't the glue that holds true connection. Growth invites people to meet you where you're going, not where you've been.

Me Moment: *Today, reflect on: Where am I playing small to avoid outgrowing a relationship dynamic? What would it feel like to trust that your growth is allowed?*

Day 225: Stepping Into More

Many of us wish for more—more time, more money, more love, more freedom. But wishing is just the beginning. Embodiment happens when you take that dream and step into it now. More freedom might mean planning a dinner out with friends. More time might mean carving out ten minutes today for a long walk. When you bring a piece of your "more" into the present, you're no longer waiting. You're living it.

Me Moment: *Choose one thing you've been wishing for more of. Ask yourself: How can I act on this desire with what I already have? Take one bold step that lets you taste your "more" right now.*

Day 226: In Their Eyes

Embodiment is about feeling connected to yourself, in the moment, in your body. It's when your inner truth matches your outer expression. When your words, your energy, and your physical presence are aligned. Fully inhabiting your spark isn't about being louder or flashier. It's about letting your full self be present without watering yourself down.

Me Moment: *Today, reflect on this:* What do I want my kids to see when they look at me? How do I want to model what it looks like to be fully myself? *Let that vision guide you toward your own embodied presence. Breathe it in. Feel it.*

Day 227: Allow It

It's one thing to want something. It's another to allow it. We can say, *I'm ready for love, money, ease*, but if we don't allow those things in, they can't land. Allowing means you stop pushing them away with doubt, fear, or old stories. It's boldly saying: *I can hold this. I deserve this. I expect this.* Wanting is passive. Allowing is powerful.

Me Moment: *Ask yourself today:* What am I truly allowing? Do I allow ease? Do I allow money to flow in? Do I allow deep friendships? *Pick one area and notice if you're letting it in or still holding it at the door.*

Day 228: Place Your Order

When you walk into a coffee shop and place your order, you don't panic about how it will show up. You trust it's on the way. You might start imagining the warmth of the cup in your hands, the smell rising up, the first sip. You even prepare by clearing the table, grabbing sugar or cream, expecting it to arrive. Your desires work the same way. Place the order, then live as if it's already yours. Expect it. Prepare for it. Act in ways that welcome it. It takes bold faith to embody the knowing that it's coming—and to move through your life from that place of trust.

Me Moment: *Write down one desire as if you're placing your order. Then ask yourself:* How would I prepare if I knew it was already mine? *Clear, shift, or gather one thing in your life today as an act of readiness.*

Day 229: Taking Up Space, Your Way

Over this past week, you've explored where you've been holding back and where you're ready to take up space with more honesty, presence, and ease. This is your reminder: taking up space doesn't require being loud or dramatic. It means being fully present in your body, your voice, your energy. You get to decide what that looks like.

Me Moment: *Ask yourself:* What does "taking up space" look like for me, right now? In my body. In my relationships. In how I show up in the world. *Write down one way you've already expanded, and one way you're excited to keep growing.*

Day 230: Bring It to Life

Dreams grow stronger when you give them texture and detail. Instead of leaving them vague—more freedom, more ease, more abundance—what if you painted them vividly? When you imagine the details and feelings of what you want, you begin aligning with it in the present. You start becoming the match.

Me Moment: *Choose one dream and describe it in rich detail. Where are you? What does it smell like, taste like, feel like in your body? What's around you, and who's with you? Let yourself dwell there for a few minutes. Notice how even imagining it impacts your outlook today.*

Day 231: Free to Be

Real confidence is the opposite of self-centredness—it's the release of constantly wondering what everyone else is thinking about you. It's the realization that you're not at the centre of everyone's story, which means you're free to live on your own terms. Free to show up as you are, unattached to how it's received. Confidence is choosing to believe in yourself, even without external proof. It's liking yourself. Backing yourself. Not because you think you're better, but because you know you're enough. It's a decision that becomes easier, and more expansive, every time you choose it.

Me Moment: *Close your eyes and tune in to the essence of confidence—not arrogance, but self-trust. Then choose one small moment to embody it today. Moving from insecurity to confidence invites you to take the focus off others and come home to yourself.*

Day 232: New Baseline

When things start feeling good—really good—it can be tempting to second-guess it, to wait for the other shoe to drop, but what if this feeling isn't a fluke? What if this is the result of all the inner work, the rewiring, the small brave choices adding up? This is what integration feels like. Your new baseline isn't a fleeting moment; it's a shift. Change happens by choosing small, aligned actions that raise your baseline, again and again, until feeling like *this* isn't rare, it's your rhythm.

Me Moment: *Close your eyes and return to a moment from the past two weeks when you felt most like your Favourite Self. Let it rise in your body. Where do you feel it? What does it feel like to trust that this isn't temporary? Breathe into it. Affirm:* This is my new baseline. I'm allowed to live here.

Day 233: Bold Rest

Boldness isn't always loud or expressive. In a world that celebrates hustle and constant striving, choosing rest is a radical act. Rest says, *I don't have to prove my worth through exhaustion. I'm allowed to nourish myself.* That's bold.

Me Moment: *Today, choose rest on purpose. Take a break without "earning it." Say no to pushing through. Whether it's five minutes of stillness or a full afternoon of a slower pace, let rest be your act of boldness today.*

Day 234: Walk the Talk

Knowing your values is one thing. Living them is another. Transformation happens when you let what matters most guide your choices—big and small. When rest is a value, you honour it with slow mornings. When freedom is a value, you make decisions from trust instead of fear. Alignment isn't perfection; it's practice.

Me Moment: *Choose one value that feels important right now. Ask: How can I embody this today? If it's care, move your body gently. If it's creativity, give yourself twenty minutes to play. If it's freedom, make one decision that reflects trust instead of fear.*

Day 235: Honouring Your Fullness

There may be parts of you that you've tried to suppress to make others more comfortable around you. Your fullness is not a liability. It's a life force. A ripple-maker. A light spreader. When you embrace it, you don't just free yourself—you expand what's possible for everyone around you.

Me Moment: *Place your hands on your heart and repeat: "I honour the vastness within me. I am safe to expand. My presence is a gift to this world." Say it until it settles. Say it until you believe it. Say it like it's always been true . . . because it is.*

Day 236: Bold Belief

You've explored what it means to take up space, to claim your desires, to lead with your presence. And when you live that way, you create a ripple of permission for others to do the same.

Me Moment: *Write about one area of your life where you've been holding back. What would bold belief in yourself look like there? Be specific—what actions would you take, what choices would you make, what conversations would you have if you led with belief instead of fear?*

Day 237

The Choice is Yours

You are not meant to run at the same pace as everyone else. Your capacity, creativity, decision-making, and rest all move to a rhythm that's uniquely yours—fast or slow, dynamic or steady—There's no "right" way, only *your* way.

In a world designed around constant, even predictable, output, it's only natural that one would lose touch with their inherent rhythm of ebb and flow. This is especially true for women. Our bodies move through yin and yang phases—through monthly cycles, seasonal shifts, and life chapters that demand different rhythms.

Trusting your rhythm means knowing when to go all in and when to pull back. It means honouring when you're "on" and when you're not, without guilt or apology. It means defining balance on your terms, not as constant moderation, but as an intuitive flow that suits who you are.

The next few weeks are about remembering how to listen. How to tune in and move at your natural pace, not the one you've been taught to chase.

When it comes to making choices, some people know in an instant. Others need to sleep on it, feel it out, ride the emotional wave until clarity arrives. Neither is better. What matters is honouring the rhythm that feels right for you. When you override your natural decision-making pace—rushing when you should take some time, hesitating when you already know what you want to do—you create tension. But when you honour your pace, even big decisions can feel peaceful.

Me Moment: *Reflect on a time when making a decision felt really good. What was the process? Fast? Slow? Intuitive? Analytical? Notice your natural rhythm. How might honouring that more often bring ease into your choices?*

Day 238: The Fear of Falling Behind

For many of us, there's a pressure that hums beneath the surface: *Keep up. Don't slow down. If you pause, you'll fall behind.* This fear can create urgency and push you to move at a pace that isn't yours—chasing timelines that don't fit, forcing output when your reserves say "not now." But your rhythm isn't wrong. Pace is personal. Slowing down or releasing urgency can be an incredibly empowering shift. It means you're syncing up with yourself.

Me Moment: *Today, notice where this fear sneaks in. Is there an area of life where you feel behind? Ask yourself: Behind compared to whom? Compared to what? How would it feel to release the race and trust your own pace?*

Day 239: Yin & Yang

Your energy has seasons. Some days you're in a yin phase—drawn inward, craving slowness, stillness, reflection. Other times, you're in a yang phase—pushing outward, active, charged up to go, create, do. Both are valuable, and both deserve to be equally honoured. The magic happens when you can read where you are and support it, not override it. Simple cues can guide you: Do you feel pulled to act, or to retreat? Are you energized, or are you craving quiet? Listening to these cues helps you stay in harmony with yourself.

Me Moment: *Today, check in: Am I in a yin or a yang phase? Notice your yearnings, your mood, your body's signals. How can you support the phase you're in, without forcing it to change?*

Day 240: JOMO—Joy of Missing Out

Not everyone recharges the same way. Some people feel alive in a busy room. Others find their restoration in solitude, and for some it's a mix of both. But we're often taught to ignore that rhythm—to say yes to every invite, to fear missing out, to believe opting out means something's wrong with us. The truth is that knowing when you need connection and when you need space is a super power. Joy of missing out happens when you trust your need for stillness, without apology.

Me Moment: *Today, reflect on how you naturally recharge. Do you feel filled up by time with others, or do you need solo space to reset? Is it consistent or does it vary depending on your season? How can you honour that rhythm this week, even in a small way?*

Day 241: Slow & Steady

Your body tells the truth about your rhythm. Tight shoulders, clenched jaw, shallow breath—these are signs of moving out of sync with yourself. But it's not just tension. Notice the pace at which you move through simple tasks. Are you rushing through the dishes? Holding your breath while you check emails? Your speed as you move through your activities reveals how tuned in you are, or aren't, to your natural rhythm. Softening your body, slowing your movements, even for a moment, can bring you back to yourself.

Me Moment: *Today, notice where your body holds tension and the speed at which you move through small tasks, then pause, unclench your jaw, relax your shoulders, and let yourself slow down. See how your nervous system responds when you change tempo.*

Day 242: The Override

From an early age, many of us are taught to stay "on"—to be productive, agreeable, available, no matter how we feel inside. Family expectations, school schedules, workplace culture . . . they all condition us to discount our inner rhythms in favour of constant output. But overriding yourself comes at a cost. Reclaim your rhythm by noticing where this pattern came from so that you can start to choose from a place of autonomy.

Me Moment: *Today, reflect on: Where did I learn to stay "on" even when my body or inner knowing asked for something else? Whose approval was I trying to keep? What patterns am I inadvertently passing on to my children?*

Day 243: Syncing Up

Over the past days, you've explored how you make decisions, how your body holds tension, how your energy moves through yin and yang phases, and how external pressures have pulled you out of sync. Every time you pause and pay attention to your body, your pace, or your desires, you deepen your connection to yourself.

Me Moment: *Take a moment to reflect on: What have I noticed about my unique rhythm lately? Maybe it's the speed at which you move, your social needs, your energetic cycles, or something else. Celebrate one small way you've honoured that rhythm and let it be proof that you can trust yourself.*

Day 244: The Pause

Not every open space needs to be filled. Not every quiet moment needs to be productive. It can be so tempting to try to fill in the gaps—saying yes because there's time, speaking up because there's silence, taking action because you feel you should—but a pause is powerful. A small break to check in with yourself: *Is this aligned with my rhythm right now?* That pause can change everything. It takes you from reacting to making a thoughtful response. From default hustle to intentional movement.

Me Moment: *Today, practice pausing before you fill a space or fill a silence. Before you add more to your plate, let the space be there. Ask yourself: Do I truly want to step into this or am I just filling space? Trust your answer.*

Day 245: Growth, Your Way

When you stay true to your rhythm, whether that means going all in or pulling back, you create sustainable and real growth. Small, aligned steps often carry you further than constant hustle ever could.

Me Moment: *Today, swap out a "more is better" habit for an aligned choice. Maybe it's crossing one thing off your to-do list that doesn't need to happen today. Maybe it's giving yourself time to do something meaningful. Allow alignment, not urgency, to set your pace.*

Day 246: Cycle Synching

Your energy isn't meant to be constant. Like nature, you move through inner seasons—times of growth, rest, creativity, and reflection. For many women, these rhythms align with their menstrual cycle. Spring (follicular): energy rises, new ideas bloom. Summer (ovulation): magnetic, social, outward-facing. Autumn (luteal): slowing down, refining, completing. Winter (menstruation): rest, reflection, inward focus. Even if you don't cycle monthly, you may feel these patterns through the moon, emotions, or life phases. Honouring them helps you work with your energy instead of against it.

Me Moment: *Today, check in: What season am I in right now? How might I align my plans, pace, or expectations with my menstrual phase? Let yourself sync with your current rhythm, whether that means doing more or doing less.*

Day 247: Reclaim your Rhythm

Ever start doing something just because it feels good, then suddenly feel the urge to monetize it? Share it? Turn it into something "useful?" Sometimes, that's true inspiration and other times, that's your rhythm being hijacked by hustle culture. It's sneaky. And it's often rooted in the belief that something only has value if it earns you money. Your natural rhythm doesn't always want to produce; sometimes it simply wants to feel. Get comfortable following the thread of what delights you without turning it into work.

Me Moment: *Think of something you love doing that brings you ease, flow, or curiosity. Now ask yourself: What would this look like if it were just for me? No posting. No perfecting. No producing. Then, make time today to do it quietly——privately. Like a love note to the present moment.*

Day 248: Move at Your Pace

Your body has its own tempo. Some days it craves flow and ease. Other days, it might want a strong, deliberate pace. Moving with intention, whether it's walking, stretching, dancing, or simply breathing deeply, helps you reconnect to your rhythm. Mindful movement is not about burning calories or "doing it right." It's about sensing your body's natural cadence and honouring how it wants to move in the moment.

Me Moment: *Today, give yourself five to ten minutes to move with presence. Walk at a pace that exactly matches your stamina. Maybe you gently stretch or sway. On the flip side, perhaps you dance or move with fierce power. Pay attention to how your body wants to move—not how you think it should. Invite today's natural cadence to lead.*

Day 249: Redo the Default

Notice your default responses. Do you typically say yes out of guilt or out of being overwhelmed? Think of when your kids ask to go outside or do something fun. Do you answer automatically, or do you check in first? Honouring your capacity matters. So does noticing when habit is leading the way. When you respond with intention, you create a life that feels honest, spacious, and true. The goal isn't to say yes more—or no more— it's to respond with awareness.

Me Moment: *Today, notice when you tend to give the same answer by default. Is there an opportunity to pause and choose differently? Practice saying yes—or no—from a place of presence, not habit.*

Day 250: Living in Harmony

You've spent time tuning in, noticing how your energy, decisions, and body all move to their own natural rhythm—not the rhythm of constant output, not someone else's pace—*yours*. Honouring that rhythm isn't a one-time thing; it's an ongoing relationship with yourself. The more you listen, the more you trust. And the more you trust, the easier it becomes to create, rest, connect, and show up in a way that feels sustainable and real.

Me Moment: *Today, reflect on one rhythm you're committed to honouring moving forward. Maybe it's how you make decisions. Maybe it's how you structure your week. Maybe it's simply trusting when you need to slow down.*

Day 251

From Criticism to Celebration

Celebration is an act of seeing. But it's also a way of being—a practice of reverence, to open your eyes to what's already here.

In these next few weeks, you'll practice letting celebration become part of your way of being—not as a finish line, but as a way of moving through life. When you honour yourself and those around you, you change how you experience the world. You tune your attention to what's working, to what's alive. Celebration creates ripple effects: rewiring your self-perception, deepening your relationships, and expanding your capacity for joy.

Critique culture, on the other hand, has led many to believe they can only improve if someone tells them what they're doing wrong. Over time, this shapes how we see ourselves: flawed, not quite enough, always needing to fix something. Not only does this impact our self-perception—it also becomes the lens through which we see others.

When we shift out of critique and into celebration, we create a brighter world for ourselves and everyone around us, especially our loved ones.

Me Moment: *Reflect on this:* How has critique culture shaped how I see myself? How has it shaped how I relate to others?

Day 252: Celebrating Her

Gossip might feel like connection in the moment, but it rarely leaves you feeling whole. It often stems from insecurity or disconnection, and while it may create a quick bond, it erodes trust, with others and with yourself. Supporting other women, on the other hand, nourishes something deeper. It strengthens your integrity. It expands what's possible, for everyone. Celebration creates momentum. Judgement stalls it.

Me Moment: *Notice the next time you're tempted to gossip about or judge another woman and pause, then choose a different path; compliment her instead, don't engage, or change the subject. Pay attention to how that choice feels in your body. The more you opt out of gossip and into celebration and support, the more you align with the version of you who uplifts, shines, and knows there's enough to go around.*

Day 253: I See You

Waiting for someone else to tell you you're doing a good job keeps your sense of worth tied to external validation. A real, lasting sense of self-worth builds when you are the first to notice your growth and successes. Your brain learns through repetition. Every time you pause to acknowledge a victory, even a tiny one, you're wiring in self-worth and expanding what you believe is possible for you.

Me Moment: *Catch yourself in a win today, big or small, and say it out loud: "I'm so proud of myself." Bonus points if you pair it with a fist pump. Notice how it feels to affirm yourself.*

Day 254: Reflecting Brilliance

Our children are constantly showing us who they are—through the questions they ask, the creations they make, and the way they move through the world. How we respond matters. Do we gloss over their excitement? Push them to do more? Or pause to celebrate the brilliance already shining through? When you reflect their light back to them, you're teaching them that who they are is enough—and that they bring something valuable to the world.

Me Moment: *Pay attention today when your child shares something with you. Instead of rushing past it or focusing on how it could be better, reflect their brilliance back. Name what you see in them— curiosity, creativity, kindness, humour. Notice how this simple practice transforms the energy in your home.*

Day 255: Hype Girl

There's something powerful about hearing your own voice. Studies even suggest the sound of your voice can be calming and healing. So what if you used it to celebrate yourself? Record a short pep talk, like you're your own biggest fan. Speak your wins out loud—big or small. Say what you're proud of, what you admire about yourself, and why you're grateful to be you.

Me Moment: *Open the voice memo app on your phone and record your pep talk. Keep it short and genuine. Save it with a title like "Hype Girl," and come back to it whenever you want to remember your own power.*

Day 256: You Don't Have to Earn It

So much of life teaches us that we only deserve to recognize our efforts after the big win, the completed project, or the perfect outcome. But you don't have to wait until everything is finished or flawless to celebrate yourself. Every small effort and choice to show up is enough to honour.

Me Moment: *Think of one small thing you did today that usually goes unnoticed—a conversation you handled with care, a task you finished even while tired, a moment you chose rest instead of pushing. Pause to celebrate it. Name it, thank yourself for it, or mark it with a small ritual. These simple acknowledgements keep you energized and remind you that your life is worth celebrating as it's happening.*

Day 257: Own Your Wins

You've spent the past week shifting from critique to celebration; learning to spot your Favourite Self in action and honouring your growth.

Me Moment: *In a sentence or two, describe how your relationship with self-recognition has evolved. What feels different now compared to where you were a week ago?*

Day 258: Self-Love Club

When you're used to showing up for everyone else, you may have a tendency to overlook what you uniquely bring to the table—your presence, your way of listening, your humour, your spark. But when you begin to see and name what's beautiful about you, you don't just boost your own confidence, you create space for others to do the same. Your self-love radiates outward.

Me Moment: *Write down three things you genuinely love about yourself—traits, qualities, ways you show up that feel true. Then next to each one, name one way that part of you impacts the people around you. Don't rush. This is a moment of seeing your own beauty with fresh eyes.*

Day 259: The Spotlight

What you choose to notice shapes your reality. Focus on flaws, and you'll find more of them. Focus on strengths, and you'll start to see potential everywhere. When you direct your attention to what's working, you're not only changing how you feel, you're also influencing your relationships, your environment, and your own sense of well-being. Every moment is a choice; amplify the problem or amplify the possibility.

Me Moment: *Next time you catch yourself ready to criticize—yourself, someone else, or a situation—pause and ask yourself: What can I celebrate here?*

Day 260: The Impact

Science confirms what we feel intuitively; emotions are contagious. According to HeartMath Institute research, the heart emits an electromagnetic field that can be measured up to several feet away. Your emotional state—calm, stressed, joyful—radiates outward and impacts others. This is why joy shifts a room. When you let yourself feel good, you generate a current that others can feel. You regulate your own nervous system and invite others into that resonance.

Me Moment: *Today, see if you can intentionally anchor into a moment of genuine joy, ease, or gratitude and feel it quietly radiating outward—to your kids, coworkers, or a complete stranger. Notice how your energy feels and how others respond.*

Day 261: You Made That!

It's almost instinctual: you create something, and your first reaction is to judge it, pick it apart, and decide it's not good enough. That reflex runs deep, and it keeps you in a loop of never feeling like you're good enough. But that can change. You can start rewiring the reflex. You can train your eyes to look for the brilliance, the power, the *you* in what you've made. It's time to pivot from critique to celebration and build a new kind of relationship with your creative self.

Me Moment: *Make something today—anything—dance, draw, take a photo, record your voice. Then take a moment and witness it with kindness. Look for what you love, even if it feels unfamiliar. Write down three things you truly appreciate about it. This is how you build a new reflex—one that knows how to honour what's real and beautiful, without needing it to be perfect.*

Day 262: A Love Letter from Your Favourite Self

It may still feel a little weird or awkward to pump yourself up, to be your own cheerleader, but what if the words of affirmation were coming from none other than your Favourite Self?

Me Moment: *Write yourself a love letter from your Favourite Self. Let her acknowledge your growth, your resilience, and your brilliance. Read it back. Soak it in.*

Day 263: Mirror, Mirror

A mirror practice involves looking into your own eyes and offering yourself compassion, affirmation, or acknowledgement. Research shows that self-directed compassion, especially when paired with visual connection, can reduce self-judgement and strengthen self-trust. What feels uncomfortable at first often softens into deep recognition. The mirror doesn't just reflect your image. It reflects the relationship you have with yourself.

Me Moment: *Spend one minute making eye contact with yourself in the mirror. Let discomfort come and go. When you feel comfortable, speak three truths about who you are.*

Day 264: You Are the Celebration

Here's the simplest truth: you are not chasing celebration; you are the celebration. Every time you honour yourself—that's you living as your Favourite Self.

Me Moment: *In a few words, describe how it feels to let yourself be the celebration. Not a moment, not an outcome—you.*

Phase Four: Live Out Loud

Welcome to the part of your journey where you expand what's already in motion—the spark you've tended, the confidence you've been embodying, the joy you've let back in. Now you get to turn up the volume. This phase invites you to savour, honour, and sustain the ways you already feel most alive.

You'll begin with Days 265 to 278, where you'll practice grounding. You'll take stock of what's already good, reassess what pulls you off centre, and learn how to bring yourself back.

Continuing into Days 279 to 292, you'll build a toolkit of rituals and practices that uniquely support your needs, well-being, and goals.

As you move into Days 293 to 306, you'll explore how your energy flows into the spaces and relationships around you. You'll play with what it feels like to be fully you—in both small and significant ways.

Progressing to Days 307 to 320, the focus shifts to connection. You'll look closely at the relationships in your life: what feels nourishing, what doesn't, and how to create a community that reflects who you are now.

In Days 321 to 334, you'll turn toward expansion. You'll practice saying yes to more pleasure, more courage, and more presence—daring to bloom bigger without waiting for perfect conditions.

To close the phase, Days 335 to 365 bring the journey full circle. You'll reflect on the ripple you've created, define what you want to carry forward, and celebrate the fact that becoming your Favourite Self isn't a finish line—it's a rhythm you now know how to return to.

Day 265

The Big Picture

These next few weeks are an invitation to land—to feel your feet on the ground of the life you're creating and catch the subtle moments that whisper, *This is it. This is good.* Grounded, attuned presence is what we're after.

When life feels overwhelming, or even just a little "off," it's easy to lump everything together and think it all needs work. But it doesn't have to be all or nothing. Looking at your life in distinct facets helps you see more clearly. It reveals what's flowing and what's stuck. You can spot patterns, notice contrasts, and understand how the different parts of your life are relating to each other.

Me Moment: *Today, reflect on these facets:*

- Love & Romance
- Friendships
- Family
- Fun & Play
- Spiritual Growth
- Finances
- Home & Environment
- Health & Energy
- Creative Expression

Rate each from 1 to 10. Which areas feel rich and nourishing? Which feel out of sync? After reflecting, choose one area that's flowing well. How can you consciously expand that mindset today and apply it to one of the facets you rated the lowest?

Day 266: Tug-of-War

Our minds are brilliant at time travel. Without even trying, our brains can jump back to replay a conversation from last week or fast-forward to next month's worries. While reflection and planning are useful, excessive time outside the present can leave us feeling scattered, anxious, or disconnected from what's happening now. Today, your only task is to pay attention: When do you find yourself drifting into the past? When does your mind race ahead into the future? What's the story you're telling yourself in those moments? When you bring yourself back to the present, you bring yourself back to your power.

Me Moment: *Notice one moment today when you've left the present, then pause, take a slow, intentional breath, and come back to what's real right now. Imagine yourself as a powerful creator present in the "now."*

Day 267: The Glimmers

Positive change can occur from amplifying what's already working well for you. Small moments of delight, ease, or connection—those are your glimmers. They're clues pointing you toward a life that feels more alive and aligned. In the noise of daily demands, it's easy to overlook them. Today, let's bring them into focus. What activities, relationships, or moments have felt expansive lately? Where do you lose track of time in the best way? Which interactions leave you feeling nourished, not drained? The more you notice these glimmers, the more space they'll naturally take up in your life.

Me Moment: *Identify three glimmers you've experienced this week. Choose one and intentionally make space for it today, even if it's just for five minutes.*

Day 268: Repeat or Reboot

Habits have a way of hardwiring themselves into your day. Maybe you wind down by staying up late to watch "just one more episode." It started as a way to relax, to carve out a little time for yourself. But at some point, it may have stopped feeling restorative and simply became routine. There is so much power in your ability to choose again. Every moment is an opportunity to take an action that aligns with how you want to feel and the life you are creating. Which habits are you repeating by default? Do they still feel aligned with how you want to live and feel?

Me Moment: *Pick one habit that you feel you've outgrown. What need was it meeting? Do you want to keep it, adjust it, or release it?*

Day 269: Reality Check

Time and money are two of your clearest mirrors. They reveal where your priorities truly land—not just what you say matters, but what you live. Maybe you say health is a priority, but your schedule is packed with everything but movement. Or you dream of creative freedom, yet most of your spending goes toward convenience and comfort. The goal here is simple: to bring your daily expenditures into harmony with what matters most to you. A reality check helps you see the gap between what you value and what you're resourcing.

Me Moment: *Look at your calendar and your recent spending. Do they reflect the life you want to create—or an old version of you? Name one small change you could make to bring them closer into alignment.*

Day 270: Dominant Intent

You choose how you look at things. Your focus directs your thoughts; thoughts shape your experience; your experience becomes your life. When you step into a moment with the intent to see beauty, connection, possibility, or progress, you don't wait for your reality to shift—you shape it. You create a future to appreciate, by appreciating the present.

Me Moment: *Set your dominant intent for the day. What do you want to see more of—kindness, synchronicity, play, ease? Say it aloud or write it down, then move through your day with eyes tuned to that frequency. Notice the impact.*

Day 271: Take a Look

You've spent the past six days noticing the shape of your current life: your habits, your focus, the ways you show up in the present moment. Today is a simple pause to take it all in.

Me Moment: *Where have you felt more connected to yourself this week? What patterns or habits have stood out?*

Day 272: The First Two Minutes

As a mum, it can be a challenge to be fully present and attuned 100 percent of the time. You've got a lot vying for your attention and that's just the reality. But profound, impactful presence can happen in small pockets of time. Practicing presence within the first few minutes of anything—drinking a glass of water, getting dressed, a simple conversation—can send a ripple of peace throughout the rest of your day.

Me Moment: *Today, you'll experiment with giving your full attention to a small moment. Notice the details: sound, texture, breath, pace. Allow yourself to experience the moment fully, without multitasking. Don't try to stretch this moment into hours. A few focused minutes can be surprisingly powerful.*

Day 273: The Power of the Pause

Reactions are fast. They often happen before you've even registered what you're feeling. But between stimulus and response, there's a sliver of space—a moment where you can choose how you want to feel and respond from that place. Over time, these tiny slivers can shape your entire reality.

Me Moment: *Today, notice a situation where you tend to react on autopilot. Maybe it's rushing to fill a silence or quickly becoming defensive. When that moment comes, pause, take a breath, and then respond in a way that feels intentional and true to you.*

Day 274: RSVP

Life is always offering small invitations—little moments that ask you to slow down, soften, or savour. A warm patch of sunlight, a song that stirs something, a stranger's unexpected kindness. Think of these like little doorways, waiting for you to notice and step through to greater sweetness. The more you tune in, the more these moments reveal themselves.

Me Moment: *Today, notice the subtle invitations around you. When life offers a moment of sweetness, pause and accept the invitation. Come in and stay a while.*

Day 275: Stop the Spiral

A bad moment doesn't equal a bad day. A tough conversation, a wave of self-doubt, a moment of overwhelm—these are just that, moments. But it's easy to let them spiral into a narrative about your whole day, your progress, or even your worth. The real power is in your ability to pause, recalibrate, and begin again—without making anything bigger than what it is. A meaningful life isn't free of challenges; it's shaped by how you respond to them.

Me Moment: *Today, if a hard moment hits, call it what it is—a moment. Take a breath. Let yourself reset without telling yourself you're failing. A hard moment can still be part of a very beautiful day.*

Day 276: Taking Stock

Taking stock of what's working helps you see just how much is already flowing in your life. From the steady beat of your heart to the clean water in your cup, your world is full of quiet, constant support. Noticing it all, even the tiniest things can shift your state in powerful ways.

Me Moment: *This isn't quite practicing gratitude; it's more like taking inventory. Set a timer for five minutes and make a list called "What's Working." Keep your pen moving—no editing, no second-guessing. Write down everything you think of; for example, my heart is beating, the fridge is stocked, my friend checked in, the sun came up—nothing is too small. Return to this practice any time you feel yourself starting to spiral.*

Day 277: Little Me

Think back to a younger version of you, the one who dreamed of feeling the way you do now. Maybe she longed for confidence, a sense of belonging, freedom, or simply peace in her own skin. Even if life isn't perfect, so many of her prayers have quietly unfolded into your present life. Today is about honouring how far you've come.

Me Moment: *Finish this sentence: Little me would be so proud of me because . . . Write as many endings as you can. Celebrate your "now."*

Day 278: To Live Fully

You've spent these past two weeks tuning in to what it means to be present—not perfectly, but with more intention. You've noticed patterns, honoured small wins, and learned how to meet yourself where you are.

Me Moment: *Take a moment to celebrate the shifts you've made and acknowledge what you want to keep growing. What part of this journey are you most proud of? And what feels exciting to continue nurturing as you move forward?*

Day 279

Your Favourite Toolkit

Living as your Favourite Self isn't a one-time breakthrough; it's a relationship. One you tend to, check in on, and nurture through small, enriching practices. Here, you will explore practices to support the meaningful life you are creating. These practices aren't about adding more to your to-do list. They're touchstones. Reminders. Ways to stay connected when life gets loud or you drift off course. Some will be playful, some grounding, some designed to pull you back to centre. And like you, they'll evolve over time.

Instead of forcing routines that feel disconnected or overwhelming, what if you created your own toolkit to help you maintain your connection to your Favourite Self—one that feels good, grounded, and true to you? Every part of your life, mind, body, heart, and spirit, deserves care. When you tune in and ask what's needed, your Favourite Self will always have something to say.

Me Moment: *Imagine your Favourite Self standing beside you, offering gentle guidance. Then, use the categories below to brainstorm a few supportive practices that feel nourishing to you.*

- *Movement (e.g., dancing, stretching, walking)*

- *Mindset (e.g., affirmations, journaling, reading)*

- *Nurturing (e.g., sleep, skincare, nourishment)*

- *Community (e.g., texting a friend, saying yes to connection)*

- *Fun (e.g., singing, dressing up, spontaneous adventures)*

Choose one to try this week. Give yourself permission to enjoy it fully.

Day 280: Opting Out

You're surrounded by messages telling you to do more, try more, be more. Ads, algorithms, and endless suggestions can make it feel like you're always behind—like the next habit, product, or system will finally make you feel complete. But what if, just for today, you tuned it all out? What if you removed the pressure to change or improve anything and chose to believe that what you're doing right now is enough?

Me Moment: *Just for today, give yourself full permission to ignore the noise; don't click on the ad, don't save the post, and don't research the thing. Unsubscribe from the pressure to optimize. You don't have to improve anything right now. Take a breath and see what it feels like to simply be here now.*

Day 281: Exploring Resistance

Sometimes you know what supports you, but actually doing it feels . . . hard. Resistance isn't failure—it's information. Often, it's your mind protecting you from discomfort, even when that discomfort is exactly what will help you grow. Today, you'll get curious about where resistance shows up, and why.

Me Moment: *Complete this sentence as many times as you can; I want to _______, but I'm worried that _______. Let your answers flow without judgement. Then, choose one small step to soften that resistance—something that gently moves you toward what you want, even if it's just a conversation, a shift in mindset, or a five-minute action.*

Day 282: The Hurdles

Even the best intentions bump into real life. You sit down to meditate and your kid needs you. A meeting runs late. You wake up with a headache. Life happens. Trying to live a hurdle-free life is unrealistic. But having a plan for how to navigate hurdles with grace is a wonderful way to support yourself. Having a backup plan (even a tiny one) keeps you connected without the all-or-nothing mindset.

Me Moment: *List out a few possible hurdles. What's a simple, flexible plan you can create for when they happen next? Give yourself an easy plan B. For example: If the kids come in while I'm meditating, I'll just invite them to join me and let it be what it is.*

Day 283: The Good Stuff

You already know what supports you. Instead of chasing the perfect self-care formula, notice what you do when you already feel good. Maybe you take a walk, turn on music, cook, or journal. These patterns are clues—they show you what helps you feel grounded and most like yourself. The truth is, you already have a built-in map to your well-being. By paying attention to these patterns, you can lean on them more intentionally—especially on the days when life feels heavier.

Me Moment: *Write down a few things you tend to do when you already feel good. Why do these feel so supportive? How could you return to them more often?*

Day 284: Return to Wonder

Somewhere along the way, many of us learned that being serious made us respectable, that depth had to be heavy, and that ease and play were signs of immaturity. But what if that's backwards? What if lightheartedness, ease, and childlike wonder aren't distractions, but signs of emotional strength? What if they're not things to grow out of, but frequencies to return to?

Me Moment: *What would it feel like to conjure up child-like wonder and cut the serious strings? First, take some time to reflect on and notice your internal bias and resistance to levity. Then, move through the world, today, as if everything is just a little bit magical. Practice awe—notice colour, texture, sunlight, sound. Practice being soft in a world that wants you hard.*

Day 285: Your Touchstones

You've spent the past days noticing the practices that support you, both in flow and in challenge. This is your moment to pause and take stock.

Me Moment: *Which small actions have you taken recently that have felt surprisingly nourishing? What new practices help you feel most connected to your Favourite Self, even on the hard days?*

Day 286: Answering the Nudge

Is there a creative pull or practice calling to you? Maybe it's morning journaling, dancing in your kitchen, signing up for a class, or revisiting a creative outlet that once lit you up. Not because it worked for someone else, but because something in you keeps circling back to it. There's often no logical reason for the tug. It doesn't shout—it hums. And still, you might keep brushing it aside, telling yourself you don't have time, or that now's not the right moment. You don't need perfect timing or permission to begin. The whisper is reason enough to start now.

Me Moment: *What practices or activities have been calling to you? Choose one and start or schedule it now.*

Day 287: Mindful Transitions

Your day is full of transitions: waking up, leaving the house, wrapping up work, stepping into parenting mode, getting ready for bed. These in-between spaces are powerful opportunities to check in and reset. A transition ritual doesn't have to be elaborate. It might be a deep breath, a moment of gratitude, or a mantra. The point is to carry your Favourite Self with you, instead of letting your life force get dragged by momentum or mood.

Me Moment: *Choose one transition in your day that tends to feel rushed or unintentional. Create a simple ritual around it—light a candle, shake it off, change your clothes, play a song. Mark the moment. Let it be a practice of presence—a practice of staying connected to you.*

Day 288: When You Fall Off Track

When you notice you've drifted from a practice you've recently started, pause, and instead of trying to force or guilt yourself back into it, ask yourself: *Is it still what I need? Does something need to shift? Or is it time to let this go?* That's it. A simple check-in to realign with what feels good and true now.

Me Moment: *Is there a practice you've lost momentum with? Reflect on it, then decide: adjust, recommit, or release. No drama, just clarity.*

Day 289: Building Self-Trust

Every time you show up for yourself, whether it's five minutes of mindful movement, a nourishing meal, or taking a breath before reacting, you're proving to yourself that you can be counted on. Small, consistent actions build self-trust over time. Not through perfection, but through presence. Today is about seeing your chosen practices as promises kept to yourself.

Me Moment: *Choose one small thing you can do today as an act of self-trust and devotion. Do it not to "be good," but to honour the kind of relationship you want with yourself.*

Day 290: Practice, but Make it Playful

It's easy to slip into "doing it right" mode with supportive practices or routines, even those you brainstormed earlier in this section. Sometimes the best thing you can do is take the pressure off. Not everything has to be serious to be meaningful. When things start to feel too serious, it may be an invitation to bring some levity in. Playfulness might look like loosening the rules, letting it be messy, or giving yourself permission to simply enjoy the moment without overthinking.

Me Moment: *Where are you overcomplicating or taking things too seriously? Choose one practice to approach with less pressure and more lightness today.*

Day 291: Integration Walk

A slow, intentional walk can be one of the most powerful ways to ground yourself into the growth you've been cultivating. As your feet meet the earth, your breath deepens, and your awareness sharpens. You're not just moving—you're integrating. An Integration Walk helps you process, embody, and live your growth, not just think about it. Let it become a regular ritual. No phone. No music. Just you, your body, and the rhythm of your own presence. Feel your pace. Notice your surroundings. You are settling into everything that's shifting within you.

Me Moment: *Take a walk today with no distractions. Move as your Favourite Self. Feel her in the way you walk, notice, breathe, and carry yourself. Imagine each step grounding you more deeply into your inner power.*

Day 292: Keep it Up

Over the past two weeks, you've explored what supports you, where you disconnect, and how to create practices that feel aligned. Now's the time to take stock of what's actually working—not just what looks good on paper, but what feels good in your life.

Me Moment: *What practice or habit feels most supportive right now? Why does it feel good? When something feels nourishing, easeful, and true to you, that's your sign to keep going.*

Day 293

On Purpose

You've already done the work of remembering who you are, reconnecting with your Favourite Self, and learning to move through life with more intention, openness, and courage. You've practiced bold embodiment—not just in curated moments, but in your real, everyday life.

Now, it's time to expand that essence even further: into your work, your relationships, and the way you show up in the world. This section isn't about becoming someone new—it's about owning who you are everywhere you go.

Your purpose isn't a job or a title. It's the unique energy you bring into the world. A blend of qualities, perspectives, and ways of being that are distinctly yours.

When you are tuned in, this essence flows through everything you touch—your conversations, your work, your relationships, even the smallest interactions. Jobs and tasks are simply vehicles. Your essence is what makes them meaningful.

Me Moment: *Reflect on the qualities and energies that feel most true to you. What's the signature blend you naturally bring to the spaces you're in? How might you share more of that essence in your daily life?*

Day 294: What They Don't See

When you're alone, or with people you trust, different parts of you naturally come forward. Maybe it's your humour, your quirks, your boldness, or your softness. Certain spaces feel safe for that version of you to show up. Other times, you might notice yourself holding back, even subtly. Today is simply about noticing what facets of you feel safe to share, and what you tend to keep private. There's nothing wrong with being discerning with what you share of yourself. Today's invitation is simply to notice how you act.

Me Moment: *Think about the version of you that shows up when you feel most safe and at ease. What do you love about her? How often does the world get to meet her?*

Day 295: Why Not You?

You might think staying muted, quiet, or small is humble. But withholding your voice, your gifts, your essence? That's not humility—it's fear wearing a disguise. You have something real to offer: a way of seeing, creating, loving, or leading that no one else can replicate. Keeping that locked away doesn't protect anyone—it deprives everyone. So ask yourself: *Why not me? Why not now?*

Me Moment: *Finish this sentence: If I fully shared my essence, the world would gain . . . Then write down what's been stopping you—and what you're ready to believe instead.*

Day 296: Safe to Be Seen

Waiting for someone to notice you keeps your power outside of yourself. But when you decide to share your voice, your ideas, or your presence on purpose, you reclaim that power. Your expression is worthy and impactful. The world is waiting for you.

Me Moment: *Today, choose one small way to be seen on purpose. Share your opinion in a meeting. Post something you care about. Wear the outfit that makes you feel magnetic. Notice how it feels to intentionally share your radiance with the world.*

Day 297: Uniquely Yours

It happens sometimes—we leave one box and accidentally step into another. You break free from being "good" and find yourself trying to be "spiritual" or "liberated" in ways that still don't feel like you. Even the idea of being "fully expressed" often comes with built-in assumptions: loud, bold, always on. These assumptions can subliminally influence so much: your clothing choices, the words you use, the music you listen to, and much more. But your version of freedom doesn't have to follow anyone else's script.

Me Moment: *What ideas have you picked up about what it means to be expressed, free, or "fully yourself?" Which of those don't fit? Define what your version of freedom feels like.*

Day 298: Own It

The parts of you that feel "big"—your ideas, creativity, opinions—are often the parts you've learned to dim. But they're also the most magnetic, the most you. True self-expression isn't about being loud—it's about being undiluted.

Me Moment: *What's one part of your personality that feels bold, bright, or expansive, but that you often tuck away? Let that part lead today. Move with self-acceptance and presence. Not just for you, but for the little eyes watching, learning how to shine.*

Day 299: Ready for More

You've uncovered a lot about how you express yourself and where your energy feels most alive. Now's a good moment to notice the next facet of your growth.

Me Moment: *What space in your life feels ready for more of your full, unapologetic presence? Describe how you'd love to show up there.*

Day 300: Break through the Ceiling

Your body holds an internal threshold for how good you believe you're allowed to feel. Joy, pleasure, ease—these aren't just emotions, they're energetic states. When they start to exceed what you're used to, your nervous system may sound the alarm: *This is a lot. Dial it down.* This is where self-sabotage sneaks in—not because you don't want to feel good, but because you've unknowingly set a ceiling on your capacity for it. Today, you'll practice (gently) breaking through that ceiling by letting your body learn that it's safe to feel good and keep feeling good.

Me Moment: *Throughout your day, whisper this to yourself, "My capacity to feel good is expanding." Say it when something delights you, when ease surprises you, when pleasure bubbles up. Wire in the truth that it really can keep getting better.*

Day 301: Your First Love

Before anyone told you to tone it down or be more realistic, there were things you did purely because they lit you up. Maybe you danced in the living room, made up stories, sang at the top of your lungs, or spent hours colouring outside the lines. That wasn't just a childhood phase—it was an early glimpse of your unfiltered, fully expressed flow. You don't need permission, talent, or a reason to bring that part of you back—you just have to want to.

Me Moment: *Think back to something you loved before you started questioning if you were good at it. What made it irresistible? What did it unlock in you? Now, bring a version of it into your life this week. Dance, draw, dress up, or play—make it yours again.*

Day 302: Showing Up Fully

There's no single way to "show up fully." For some, it's taking the lead in a room. For others, it's saying no without apology. Sometimes, it's simply allowing yourself to be seen without shrinking. What matters is how it feels for you when you're fully yourself and standing in your power. This is your opportunity to claim that definition—on your terms.

Me Moment: *How would you describe what it feels like to show up fully as yourself? What does it look like in different facets of your life— motherhood, relationships, work? Write your own definition that feels true and grounded.*

Day 303: Mama Mirror

Relationships can be powerful mirrors. Nowhere is this truer than in motherhood. The way you show up for your children reflects so much about how you're showing up for yourself. Your patience, your boundaries, your joy, even your frustration—it's all information. Every interaction is a chance to better understand your own patterns, needs, and growth.

Me Moment: *Think of one interaction with your child that stands out—whether it felt rewarding or challenging. If it feels helpful, reflect on both types of moments. What did that moment reveal about you? What did you notice about your own tendencies?*

Day 304: Small Moments

You don't need a stage or a special moment to show up as your Favourite Self. The way you greet a neighbour, converse with a cashier, or respond to a text message is an opportunity to bring more of you into the world. These small moments shape how you feel in your own life. The more often you meet them with your full self, the more natural it becomes.

Me Moment: *As you move through today, choose one ordinary interaction—a quick conversation, an errand, a passing hello. Notice how it feels to show up as your Favourite Self, even in something small.*

Day 305: Put It Down

There's power in deciding what you're done trying to prove. In the letting go of the pressure to be palatable, productive, perfect. In the letting go of the urge to prove you're enough by betraying your own inner knowing. Sometimes, the bravest thing you can do is put it down. Release the weight of roles you never chose. Let go of striving that no longer fits. You don't have to earn your worth. You just have to own your truth.

Me Moment: *What are you done trying to prove? What's felt forced, heavy, or like it belonged to someone else's idea of success? Write it down. Then say it aloud: "I'm putting this down." Let the relief rise. Let it be real.*

Day 306: This Is What It Feels Like

Over the last two weeks, you've explored how you move through the world: where you expand, where you hold back, and how you want to show up. Living as your whole true self is a feeling you create. A way of being that unfolds as you stay connected to yourself. Today, you'll give words to that feeling.

Me Moment: *In your own words, describe what it feels like to live as your fully expressed Favourite Self. Not an ideal, just what feels true right now. Let this serve as a touchstone you can return to.*

Day 307

Who Feels Like Home

You are not meant to live in isolation. The people you surround yourself with—the ones who see you, uplift you, challenge you, and grow with you—shape your experience just as much as you shape theirs. When you focus on relationships that feel meaningful, aligned, and true to who you are now, life becomes fuller

In the next few weeks, you'll explore how relationships reflect your growth, how you respond in different dynamics, and what you truly crave in community. You'll also get clear on the roles you want to play and let go of the ones you've outgrown.

You're creating connections that feel nourishing, honest, and alive; rooted in your truth. This section invites you to be intentional about the relationships you choose to grow and the energy you bring to them.

There are people who make you feel at ease the moment you're with them. With them, there's no performing, no adjusting, you just breathe a little deeper and you sound more like yourself. These are the connections that feel like home, not because they're perfect, but because you feel safe to bring your whole self to the table.

Me Moment: *Reflect on how you feel in relationships where you're fully yourself and ask yourself: What words come to mind? What does this tell you about the types of connections you want to nurture more of in your life?*

Day 308: Who Lifts, Who Drains

Every interaction leaves an imprint. Some people energize you, spark ideas, or leave you feeling lighter. Others might leave you feeling tense, depleted, or off-centre. And some may leave you feeling completely neutral. Noticing how you feel after an exchange helps you understand what supports you and what doesn't. That awareness gives you choice.

Me Moment: *Reflect on the people and spaces that feel uplifting and energizing for you: Where or with whom do you leave feeling more like yourself versus drained and disconnected? Your body's responses can serve as a powerful guide.*

Day 309: Roles You've Outgrown

There may be relationships where you automatically take on certain roles: The fixer. The peacekeeper. The entertainer. The strong one. Some of these roles are chosen. Others were picked up along the way, shaped by family, work, or past versions of yourself. It's time to notice which roles feel true to you now, and which ones feel like they no longer fit.

Me Moment: *Reflect on a role you often find yourself playing in certain relationships. Does it still feel authentic? Or are you ready to step into something that feels more aligned with who you are today?*

Day 310: When Growth Creates Distance

As you grow, some relationships evolve with you . . . and others don't. That doesn't make them bad or wrong—it just means you're in a different season. Some connections are meant for your whole story, while others are there for a chapter, but both can be valuable.

Me Moment: *Think of a relationship or dynamic that feels harder to maintain as you grow. What has shifted in you? What does that reveal about the kind of connection you're craving now and what you're ready to release?*

Day 311: Belonging Feels Different

There's a relief that comes with true belonging. You don't have to mask, edit, or prove yourself. You're just . . . welcome. Fitting in, on the other hand, often asks you to adjust, to perform, or to stay small to stay accepted. The difference isn't always obvious until you stop and feel it.

Me Moment: *Reflect on a space or relationship where you feel a deep sense of belonging. How might you offer that same sense of welcome to someone else?*

Day 312: What You're Really Looking For

When it comes to connection, we often slip into old patterns—maintaining relationships out of habit or accepting surface-level interactions simply because they're familiar. But you're allowed to want more: more depth, lightness, play, support, and authenticity. The blend is yours to define. Getting clear on what you truly want in your relationships helps you recognize it when you see it and create it when you don't.

Me Moment: *What qualities do you want to have in your friendships, community, and relationships? Name what you're truly looking for and how you might start creating more of that in your world?*

Day 313: Recalibrating Community

Over the past six days, you've looked at how relationships shape your well-being, the roles you tend to step into, the difference between belonging and fitting in, and what you truly crave in connection. You've named the spaces where you feel free to be yourself and the ones that push you to shrink or adjust. Now is your chance to step back and see what all of this is showing you.

Me Moment: *Note the relationship patterns you've uncovered. Where do you feel most supported and seen? Where are you feeling the urge to change, release, or reimagine how you connect? What does this reveal about the kind of community you want to build moving forward?*

Day 314: Be the Energy You Seek

The connections you crave begin with how *you* choose to show up. When you radiate the qualities you seek in connections, you make it easier for like-hearted people to find you. You don't have to wait for someone else to go first.

Me Moment: *Choose one quality you wish you felt more of in your relationships. Today, explore how you can bring a small spark of that energy into your interactions—starting with yourself.*

Day 315: Brave Invitations

Meaningful connection often starts with a small invitation: a text to check in, a coffee date, a genuine comment that opens the door to something deeper. Reaching out can make you feel vulnerable. Not every invitation will be received the way you hope, and that's okay. What matters is that you're leading from a place of alignment, not obligation.

Me Moment: *Think of one person you'd like to get to know better or with whom you'd like to deepen your relationship. What's a small, low-pressure invitation you could extend to them? Reach out and see what happens.*

Day 316: Boundaries Are Connection Too

Healthy boundaries aren't walls. They're bridges—creating clear, honest spaces where real connection can happen. When you honour what feels true and sustainable for you, you're also showing up more authentically for others. You're choosing honesty over resentment and clarity over guessing games. Boundaries are an act of care for you and your relationships.

Me Moment: *Reflect on a relationship or dynamic where you feel stretched thin. What's one small boundary you could honour that would support a deeper, healthier connection?*

Day 317: Not That Girl

You know the one. The girl you've judged. The one who says what she means. The one who celebrates her wins out loud. The one who walks into a room like she belongs. Somewhere along the way, you were taught that being her was dangerous—or at least distasteful. Maybe you rolled your eyes. Maybe you told yourself, *I'm not like that*. But what if that judgement wasn't really about her at all? What if it was about a part of you that wanted permission?

Me Moment: *Today, reflect on the type of woman you've been conditioned to avoid being. Think back to a time when you labelled another woman as "too (something)"—too loud, too emotional, etc. What about her rubbed you the wrong way? This isn't about guilt— it's about curiosity. Name one quality in "that girl." Ask yourself: What would it look like if I let a little of my own version of that live in me?*

Day 318: Mama Magic

Routines can be essential in motherhood—they create rhythm, structure, and flow, but within that rhythm, there's often a tendency to fall out of presence and into autopilot. Some of the sweetest moments of connection happen when you pause, get curious, and meet your child in their world. You don't need a big "quality time" plan. Sometimes it's as simple as really listening, asking one more question, or letting yourself be playful with them.

Me Moment: *Choose one moment today, such as bedtime, the ride home, or a quick chat, to be fully present with your child. Follow their lead. This is your chance to experience connection, not just manage the moment. It's not an extra to-do on your list, just a simple shift in perspective.*

Day 319: Savour the Sweetness

One of the simplest ways to nurture connection is through shared joy— laughing together, geeking out over a common interest, or letting a silly moment be just that: silly. These small bursts of joy create bonds that don't need deep conversations to be meaningful. When you give yourself permission to enjoy, you invite others to do the same.

Me Moment: *Notice a moment today when joy shows up: whether it's a joke, a shared look, or a small celebration. See if you can soften into it, breathe it in, and let it expand just a little more.*

Day 320: You, Connected

Over the past two weeks, you've explored how relationships influence your energy, the kinds of connections you desire, and what feels truly nourishing in community. You've noticed where you belong, where you dim your light, and how you can embody the qualities that you wish to receive. This reflection is your chance to ground into what you've discovered and how you want to keep showing up in your connections.

Me Moment: *Think about how you feel when you're connected to others as your Favourite Self. What kind of relationships light you up? How do you want to keep cultivating that feeling in your life?*

Day 321

You Made It Here

You've laid the groundwork. You've rooted, stretched, and softened. Now? It's time to rise. This section is where you dare to bloom bigger. It's time to say yes to what brings you alive. It's time to flirt with pleasure, play with vision, and expand into the fullest version of your Favourite Self—not just in theory, but in real life.

Full bloom is making bold moves, trusting your glow, and showing up like you belong in the life you're creating. Remember, blooming isn't a finish line; it's a rhythm you get to return to, again and again.

Blooming doesn't always look like fireworks and celebration. Sometimes it looks like showing up when you'd rather hide, choosing gentleness when things feel heavy, or trusting the process more than you doubt. Let's explore what it means to bloom for you.

Me Moment: *Write yourself a blessing for exactly where you are today. Whether you feel in bloom or still underground, what words would feel grounding, encouraging, or true like nourishment and sunlight?*

Day 322: Magnetism

Every so often, life hands you a flash of knowing—when the air feels charged, your chest opens, and you know in your bones you're exactly where you need to be. These aren't accidents. They're guideposts. They remind you what it feels like to be lit from within.

Me Moment: *Recall a recent moment when you felt fully alive, like the world and your spirit were moving in sync. Spend a few minutes conjuring up that feeling and let it sink in. Stretch the feeling through your whole body. Let it linger. This feeling is your natural state—the place you magnetize from.*

Day 323: Quiet Growth

Growth doesn't always look like a new habit or a bold move forward. Sometimes, it shows up in what you no longer carry. Perhaps you don't spiral the way you used to, or you don't over apologize, overextend, or hold so tightly to being perfect. Maybe you take a breath instead of reacting without pause, or maybe you rest without feeling guilt.

Me Moment: *What's one reaction, behaviour, or pattern you've quietly released? Something you've stepped out of, even if no one noticed. Name it and honour the space it's made for something new.*

Day 324: The Bloom and The Burn

Every chapter of growth brings both beauty and shedding. There are things you've grown into—new ways of thinking, being, and showing up. At the same time, there are things you've let go of—habits, expectations, or identities that no longer fit. Both types of changes deserve recognition. You don't need to label it all as good or bad. Some things bloomed while others have burned. That's part of becoming.

Me Moment: *Write a short "bless and release" letter to this season of your life. Name what you're grateful for that bloomed. Name what needed to fall away. Thank both for shaping you.*

Day 325: Already Enough

You are not a project. You are not a rough draft waiting to be perfected. You're a person—and this version of you deserves to be honoured, not constantly edited. Growth has its place, but so does presence. So does wholeness. So does claiming joy in the life you've built today.

Me Moment: *Ask yourself: Where have I been treating myself like something to fix? Name one belief, habit, or pressure you're ready to cut loose. Then say out loud: "I am enough, exactly as I am."*

Day 326: The Space Between

You're not the same person who began this journey; the way you speak to yourself, move through your day, and trust your voice may have all changed. Even so, some things may feel tender. Your dreams may stir nerves or doubt. That doesn't mean you're not ready; it means you're pushing against the edges of your identity.

Me Moment: *Name one thing you're proud of about who you've become. Then, name one thing that still feels far away. What might shift if you met both with the same love?*

Day 327: The View from Here

When you zoom out, patterns begin to emerge. Moments that once felt random start to connect. You can see the path you carved, not by force, but by presence—step by step. Some days were subtle, and some cracked you wide open, but all of them brought you here.

Me Moment: *Take a moment to look at the journey behind you. What are you proud of? What surprised you? What would you whisper to the version of you who started this chapter*

Day 328: The Art of Reverence

Reverence multiplies what you're given. It slows you down just enough to say, *This matters*. It turns ordinary moments into captivating ones. Think of it like this: You prepare a snack for each of your kids. One throws it on the floor. One scarfs it down without a word and leaves you crumbs. But the third? They smile, savour it, and say thank you. Who do you want to make another snack for? The universe responds to reverence the same way.

Me Moment: *How can you bring more reverence into your day today? It could be savouring the morning sunlight, leaning into a conversation, or fist pumping into the air after a small win. No matter what your answer is, be present. Then ask yourself: How can I bring more of this quality into the way I move through life?*

Day 329: Pleasure Is Power

Pleasure isn't the same as happiness or joy. It's an embodied experience—a full-sensory *yes*. It lives in the body, not the mind. For many women, pleasure has been framed as indulgent, selfish, or unnecessary. We're taught to deny it, minimize it, or feel guilty for wanting it. But research shows that the opposite of pleasure isn't pain—it's powerlessness. When we are disconnected from pleasure, especially our ability to create it for ourselves, we often feel ungrounded, depleted, or numb. Pleasure is personal power. It wakes up the body, reconnects us to our spark, and affirms that our experience matters.

Me Moment: *When you feel a sense of powerlessness, tune in to pleasure. Shift your focus from the story in your mind to your physical senses. What would bring you back into your body right now? Maybe it's warmth, rhythm, taste, texture, or breath. Choose one simple, sensual act that reconnects you to yourself, and let it remind you that your body, your experience, and your spark belong to you.*

Day 330: Rise Up

As we've explored in earlier sections, growth isn't about trying to avoid the low moments. They'll come. What changes is how you meet them. Instead of spiraling, you recover faster. Instead of collapsing, you steady yourself sooner. This is resilience: the ability to rise again without losing yourself in the wobble.

Me Moment: *Think of a recent moment that once would have derailed you—but didn't. Name the shift—emotionally, mentally, or behaviourally—that shows your new capacity.*

Day 331: I Am

Your words are instruction. Every time you say "*I am,*" your brain listens. Your body listens. Your cells respond. It's common to say things like "*I'm a mess,*" or "*I'm behind,*" without thinking twice. But try saying "*I am radiant,*" or "*I am powerful,*" and it might feel uncomfortable. That's because you've had more practice saying and believing the negative. This is how identity forms and how it evolves. The more clearly you affirm what's true and powerful, the easier it becomes to live that way.

Me Moment: *Complete the sentence: I am . . . Choose a truth you're ready to embody. Say it out loud. Say it like it matters, because it does.*

Day 332: Evidence, Not Competition

When you witness someone thriving, what comes up for you? Inspiration, jealousy, a hushed *I wish?* These reactions are signals. What you admire is often a mirror—reflecting a part of you that's ready to be seen. If someone's light stings, maybe you're dimming your own. Not everyone's success may trigger you, but when it does, there's usually a reason. It's asking you to pay attention.

Me Moment: *Think of someone whose life has stirred something in you. Instead of turning away, ask, What part of me is she waking up?*

Day 333: Your Becoming Ceremony

If someone you love shared a win or a powerful realization, you'd pause, witness, and celebrate it. You deserve the same.

Me Moment: *Take time to create a ceremony for yourself sometime this week: light a candle, dress up, journal, dance, or speak out loud. Choose elements that feel personal and let them reflect the energy you want to carry forward. You might want to include your kids too!*

Day 334: Full Bloom

You don't have to feel "done" to be in full bloom. You just need to feel rooted in your truth, aligned with your essence, and connected to your life force. Blooming isn't a peak—it's a rhythm. It's showing up as yourself and letting that be enough.

Me Moment: *What does full bloom feel like for you right now? What's changed in how you see yourself, and what are you taking with you into whatever comes next? If it feels good, draw or paint a representation of this season of your life.*

Day 335

The Ripple Effect

This is the last category in the final phase of your journey—a space devoted to honouring how far you've come and integrating what you've learned, thus it has more days than the previous categories. You're not just learning new ideas; you're living them, and that deserves space.

You've spent the past year waking up, expanding into joy, reclaiming your voice, and reconnecting with the truest parts of yourself. You didn't just read a book—you lived it. You showed up when it was hard. You dared to imagine a life that feels like you. You celebrated the small shifts.

Now it's time to take stock of what those shifts have created—not just within you, but around you. This section will help you look clearly at the ripple you're creating, stretch gently toward what's next, and carry it all forward with more clarity, intention, and trust.

Your legacy doesn't get made in the future. It's taking root now—today. It's how you speak. It's how you hold your child when they're melting down. It's how you treat yourself in front of the mirror. It's how you take up space and show the world who you are.

When you're rooted in who you are, other people feel it. You're not bending over backwards. You're not being "nice" to keep the peace. You're just being *you*, and that releases the pressure for others to perform too. Your presence becomes an invitation: to exhale, to be real, to feel safe.

Me Moment: *Reflect on how your self-acceptance has impacted your relationships—with your children, romantic relationships, your friends, your family, your work. What feels different now? Where has your growth made space for something better?*

Day 336: You're Already Leading

Whether you believe it or not, you are a leader. Every time you model a boundary, make a hard decision, regulate your emotions, or stand in your truth, you're leading by example. You influence the energy of your home, your relationships, your work, and your community. Leadership isn't about having all the answers. It's about showing up in a way that empowers others—and you've been showing up in ways that matter.

Me Moment: *Reflect on how you've led this year through example, presence, or action. Then ask yourself: Where are you being invited to step into more leadership? What spaces can benefit from your gifts, talents, and strengths?*

Day 337: Carry Yourself Forward

You communicate who you are long before you say a word. It's in your posture. Your eye contact. The way you enter a room, stay in a moment, or leave one. How you carry yourself reflects how you see yourself and how others experience you.

Me Moment: *How has the way you carry yourself changed this year? What does your presence say before you speak? And how would you like it to feel, moving forward?*

Day 338: Lasting Impression

Think about your eulogy; yes, it's a little morbid, but it's clarifying. People won't remember you for how much you crossed off your to-do list. They'll remember how you made them feel. Your presence leaves an imprint. It speaks louder than your accomplishments.

Me Moment: *How do you want people to feel in your presence and after you leave the room? What emotional impact do you want to have on your kids, your loved ones, your community? Define the way of being you want to be remembered for.*

Day 339: Not Your Story

There are so many ideas handed to women about what a meaningful life should look like: be nurturing, be ambitious but not too assertive, make time for everyone but still take care of yourself, leave a mark but not in a way that makes anyone uncomfortable. It's exhausting. These narratives are often not even yours; you've absorbed them from others. Now, you get to define what a meaningful life looks like. You get to decide what legacy means—for you.

Me Moment: *What messages have you absorbed about the kind of woman, mum, or leader you should be? What expectations have shaped your idea of "success" or "enough?" Cross out what's not yours. Keep what feels true.*

Day 340: Stretching into What's Next

Sometimes you can feel the next chapter stirring before you can name it. You feel the nudge, the idea, the urge to expand. But with expansion often comes friction—old fears, new doubts, and stories about why it's not the right time. This may be signaling that you are at the edge of your next stretch.

Me Moment: *What do you feel yourself being pulled toward? What's calling you forward, and what still tries to hold you back? Be honest about both. Remember: growth isn't linear, and there is no pinnacle. You're good enough as you are, and you are allowed to evolve without guilt.*

Day 341: The Next Chapter

You've come a long way—in what you've already done and in how you see yourself, what you tolerate, and what you're dreaming of doing next.

Me Moment: *What are you proud of from this chapter of your life? And as you look ahead, what are you now ready to imagine for yourself?*

Day 342: Reverse Legacy

Imagine your child growing up and adopting your current habits, beliefs, or ways of being. What would you want them to carry forward? What would you want them to release? Generational change begins with awareness, followed by one small shift at a time.

Me Moment: *Reflect on the beliefs, habits, or thought patterns you're passing on, intentionally or not. What do you feel proud to hand down? What would you choose to rewrite, starting now?*

Day 343: Future Self Check-In

Today, write an encouraging note to yourself: a reminder of your power, your truth, and the essence that makes you who you are. Put that note in a drawer, a journal, or tucked inside a book, or somewhere else you'll remember.

Me Moment: *Open your calendar and choose a future date—maybe a few weeks from now, a few months, or even a year. Add a reminder to read the note. You're leaving a hidden gem of wisdom and love for your future self to discover. A secret "I've got you" tucked into time.*

Day 344: Your Guiding Words

How do you want to feel moving forward? Instead of focusing on hard and fast goals, think about a few words that encapsulate the life you are building. These words don't need to impress anyone. They just need to feel true. Choose them not to fix yourself, but to guide you back when things get noisy.

Me Moment: *Choose one to three words that will serve as your North Star for this next chapter of your life. Then, if you're feeling crafty, create something visual with these three words. Think of this like creating a vision board, but instead of images, you're choosing words. Not goals or tasks, but the energy you want to walk in. Words that feel like a return to your essence.*

Day 345: Pass It On

Every time you break a pattern, speak your truth, rest without guilt, or model joy, you're passing something on. Maybe it's how you handle hard emotions in front of your kids. Maybe it's the way you cheer for your friends instead of competing. In these moments, you are modelling something powerful to your children—what it looks like to live in alignment with your truth.

Me Moment: *What's something you've practiced or reclaimed this year that you hope your children, your friends, and your community witness or feel from you? How can you pass it on through how you show up?*

Day 346: No More Commiserating

Part of your growth means stepping out of conversations that keep you tethered to old identities. There's a difference between being a safe space and commiserating to make others comfortable. You don't have to keep participating in conversations you've outgrown. Instead, you can hold space for others to release frustrations while reflecting and reminding them of their power.

Me Moment: *Where are you ready to stop reinforcing storylines that no longer feel true, even if it's subtle? How can you do this in a way that feels aligned with your desires and intention around community and connection?*

Day 347: Living Proof

You don't have to convince anyone you've changed. You don't need a speech, a post, or external validation to prove you're growing. The way you move through the world now—the way you speak, choose, pause, and show up, that's living proof. Let your life reflect your evolution—quietly, boldly, however it wants to move through you.

Me Moment: *Where have you felt the urge to explain or prove your growth? What would it feel like to release that and simply live it instead?*

Day 348: The Life You're Creating

Pausing to take inventory of your life helps you see the patterns, name what matters, and notice what's working so you can keep building with intention.

Me Moment: *What does the life you're creating feel like today? What are you proud to be growing, and what truth do you want to stay rooted in as you move forward?*

Day 349: Feel the Spark

Feeling fully turned on to life and alive doesn't look or feel the same for everyone. For you, it might feel calm. For someone else, it might feel playful or bold. For most, that feeling will shift and evolve according to their season of life. What matters is noticing what *your* version feels like in your body and in your daily life—and trusting that it's enough.

Me Moment: *Write your own definition of what it feels like to be alive and tapped in. Use words that feel true in your body—fizzy, grounded, lit up, soft, strong. Then keep a light radar out today: Where does that feeling show up? What moments bring even I percent more aliveness?*

Day 350: Life Alignment

Living in alignment is not about everything being perfect. It's about feeling like you're living your life and not just performing in it. Maybe things are still messy. But underneath that, there's a shift. You have more ease, more honesty, and more days where your life feels like a reflection of who you really are.

Me Moment: *Look at your current life through the lens of alignment. What feels more you now than it did when you started? Maybe it's a habit, a boundary, a feeling in your body. Make a list of three to five ways your life feels more yours now.*

Day 351: She Got You Here

When we go through a transformational journey, there's a tendency to look back and see who we were "before." Like we've outgrown her. Like we've arrived somewhere better. But that's not fair to the person you were. You're here because *she* was brave. She was the one who noticed something wasn't right. She was the one who said *enough*. She kept showing up, even when it was hard, even when it was messy. Eventually, she gave herself to you—she surrendered, she softened, and she did the work.

Me Moment: *Today, write a thank-you to the version of you who got you here. Let her know you see her clearly now. Name what you admire. This is not a goodbye to her—this is a bow of reverence.*

Day 352: Be a Joy Magnet

Throughout the past year, you've learned that joy is a frequency you can tune into. The more you notice it, the more it expands. Joy lives in what's already beautiful, already working, already shimmering in your ordinary moments. When you tune into that, you don't just feel joy, you attract more of it. It's as though your joy receptors are more open and more available to take in what's already here.

Me Moment: *Today, practice being a joy magnet. Look for beauty, softness, surprise. Let yourself notice it without feeling like you have to earn it. Be present to what sparks a flicker of delight and let yourself receive it fully.*

Day 353: A New Kind of Fun

As you grow, your definition of fun may change. What once felt exciting may now feel draining. What the mainstream world calls fun might overstimulate your nervous system or just not land anymore, and that's not a problem. That's clarity. You're allowed to want slower joy, quieter pleasure, or a version of fun that makes no sense to anyone but you. You don't owe anyone an explanation for what fills you up now.

Me Moment: *What feels like fun for this version of you? Make a short list of things that feel nourishing, playful, or light, and try one today or begin seeking one out. Don't be shy about recruiting your people to engage in new ways of fun with you.*

Day 354: Shine On

You've softened, expanded, experimented, and remembered who you are. Now, you're ready for the stretch. This is your permission to go even deeper into self-expression—to live more freely, care less, follow your sparks, and let your truth lead.

Me Moment: *Think of one area in your life where you're fully yourself. Now choose an area where you still feel a little held back. What mindset helps you shine in the first area? Is it caring less what people think? Trusting your voice? Letting go of the outcome? Write it down. Then ask: How can I carry that same mindset into the space that still feels tight? Use the answer to take one simple action in the area where you feel held back. Try it today even in a small way.*

Day 355: The Art of Living Life Well

Living life well is an art, and you are the artist. It's the act of crafting a life that feels rich with meaning, beauty, and presence. The art of living life well might show up in how you get dressed, how you make your tea, how you speak to yourself, how you move through a room. It's expressed in the tiny details, the textures of your day, the choices you make on purpose. And like any art form, it's allowed to evolve.

Me Moment: *What does the art of living life well look like for you? Choose one area of your day—morning routine, cooking, movement, how you transition between tasks—and treat it like an art form.*

Day 356: Forward Momentum

Attaching to a specific outcome can feel empowering at first, like clarity, like vision. But over time, it can start to tighten. You may notice the tension of control, the pressure to make it happen, or the anxiety that builds when things don't land exactly how you imagined. There's another way to stay connected to your desires. One that feels lighter, more sustainable, and more rooted in trust. You can choose to create momentum instead of gripping. Every time you pivot your focus from fixation to flow, you support your future self.

Me Moment: *Take a moment to picture your future self—she might be days, weeks, years ahead or mere moments into the future. Now, imagine your current self sending a wave of support toward her, not to control what happens, but to energize the path she's walking. Use this practice anytime you feel yourself clinging.*

Day 357: The Chapters

Your story isn't linear—it's layered. And when you look back, the shifts might not show up in words . . . but they might show up in your face, your eyes, your posture, your presence. You can often see your becoming before you can name it.

Me Moment: *Scroll through the photos in your phone, month by month, starting from the beginning of this journey. Choose one photo from each month that stands out to you. Name each month like a chapter, using the photos as inspiration. Give them titles that reflect the essence you carried, released, or discovered. This becomes a visual record of your becoming.*

Day 358: Date Night!

Let's mark this moment with a celebration! A real one. You've shown up for yourself in so many ways. Now it's time to show up big! Take yourself out. Alone, with a partner, or with your favourite people. Dress in a way that feels like your Favourite Self. Order the thing that lights you up. Drape yourself in sparkle, shine, and laughter. Dazzle on purpose. It's time to show off your spark!

Me Moment: *Plan an outing to honour this chapter. It can be simple or extra. Decide what you'll wear, where you'll go, and how you'll show up. Go all in. Be a walking reminder that joy belongs to you.*

Day 359: Hold Your Energy

Now comes the deeper invitation—to stay rooted in your truth and vitality even when others don't fully see you. Not everyone will get it. Some people are used to an older version of you. Some might never fully understand what's changed. But you don't have to prove anything. You don't have to hold back either. You just get to hold your energy. Let it speak for itself.

Me Moment: *Write down the names of one or two people who are close to you but may not fully see or celebrate your evolution. Then brainstorm one way you can stay grounded in your presence around them, not to convince them, but to stay connected to you. Think about your tone, posture, boundaries, humour, or softness. What does holding your energy look like in practice?*

FULL CIRCLE

Day 360: Dare to be Wrong

There's a belief so many of us carry—quiet, deep, persistent—that we have to get it right. That we'll only be worthy if we do it the "correct" way. But what if the most freeing thing you could do . . . is do it "wrong?" What if you went off-script on purpose? When you break a small, made-up rule and see that nothing bad happens, you start to rewire your brain. You teach your body that *I'm safe to do it my way*. Not every rule is meant to be broken; green means go, red means stop, but when it comes to self-expression? You get to decide. You don't have to fit into someone else's mold to be okay.

Me Moment: *Do something today that challenges the idea that you have to get it right. Go to the grocery store overdressed. Take a dance class and add your own flair. Pause in a moment you'd normally try to perfect. Recalibrate your nervous system so it understands that you are safe to show up as you are.*

Day 361: Be Your Own Witness

Take a moment to honour the woman who kept showing up. Think back to where you were when you began this journey—how you felt, what you believed, what you hoped might change. Now, stand here in this moment and witness yourself. Not through the lens of what's still unfinished, but through the truth of how much you've lived, remembered, and reclaimed. This is a moment of celebration, reverence, and recognition.

Me Moment: *This evening before bed, stand in front of the mirror. Look into your own eyes and take yourself in. Say aloud or silently, "I see you. I honour you. You are magnificent." Breathe it in. Feel the truth of those words. Receive them fully.*

Day 362: A Year of Becoming

This journey was never really about becoming a new you. It was about becoming the most you. Day by day, choice by choice, you remembered your voice. You followed the spark. You let go of the pressure to be perfect and chose to be present instead. That's what becoming really is. It's not a finish line, but a return to your essence—lived out loud.

Me Moment: *Write a few sentences that describe who you are at your core. Not your job or your roles, but your truest energetic signature.. How do you carry yourself? How do you feel in your skin? What do you know about yourself now that you didn't before?*

Day 363: Keep Saying Yes

You've said yes in a hundred small ways: yes to joy, yes to softness, yes to showing up when it would've been easier to shut down, yes to something more, and you don't have to stop now. The story doesn't end here. It will continue to come alive in your daily choices, in how you move through your mornings, how you speak to yourself, and how you show up for what matters.

Me Moment: *Write down three things you want to keep saying yes to. They don't have to be big, they just have to feel true. Keep this list somewhere you'll see, as a gentle reminder that you get to keep choosing a life that feels like it's yours.*

Day 364: Pay It Forward

This journey hasn't just changed how you see yourself; it's changed how you show up in the world. You've become someone who walks with more presence, more joy, more light. Someone who leads by living. You are the celebration—not because of what you've accomplished, but because of how you now embody your energy and care for your life-force. And now, it's time to pay it forward.

Me Moment: *Think of someone who would benefit from remembering her Favourite Self—a friend, a sister, a new mum, a coworker, someone you love or someone you barely know. When you're ready, pay it forward by reflecting back to her what you see: a genuine compliment, a reminder of her brilliance, a celebration of who she already is. Let the current move through you to someone else who's ready to remember herself too.*

Day 365: Mindfully You

You made it! Not just to the end of this book, but to a deeper relationship with yourself—one built on joy, truth, curiosity, courage, softness, and spark. You are not who you were when you started—but you're not someone else either. You are more *you* than ever, and that's the point. There will be days ahead that feel messy or flat, and that's okay. Your spark doesn't want perfection; it just wants your attention. As you move forward, you are invited to stay in playful conversation with what makes you feel awake and real and fully here.

Me Moment: *Stand in front of the mirror. Look at the woman who kept showing up. Say, "Thank you, I love you." Then write a manifesto—not for the world, but for yourself. One sentence. One truth. One promise. Tape it to the mirror. This is your signature. This is your exclamation point.*

The Mindful Mum Way

Look at how far you've come. From those first quiet sparks in *Phase One: Wake the Wild*, to standing fully in your power in *Phase Four: Live Out Loud*, you've returned to the truth of who you are. This was never about becoming someone new. It was about remembering. Reclaiming. Rooting into the version of you that feels most alive.

You've moved through a full spectrum of emotions and experiences—and that's what makes this real. The ups and downs, the joy and doubt, the resistance and release . . . it all belongs. You now have tools, awareness, and language to meet yourself in any season and to keep choosing the life that feels most *you*.

There will be more seasons. More shifts. More invitations to rise, rest, and reawaken. Your Favourite Self isn't fixed—she evolves. That's the beauty of living fully. You don't have to get it right. You just have to keep coming home.

So when things feel off, come back. Re-read an entry. Dance to your playlist. Plan a solo date. Say something out loud that makes you feel like you.

Keep saying yes to the life that wants you in it. You are vibrant. You are awake. You are alive again.

This isn't the end. It's your next beginning.

Keep going. Keep glowing. Keep choosing you.

Resources

Here are the books, tools, and teachers to go deeper with what lit you up.

Books:

Burnout by Emily and Amelia Nagoski

How Do You Choose? by Erin Claire Jones

MyFlo by Alisa Vitti

Self-Compassion by Dr. Kristin Neff.

The Artist's Way by Julia Cameron.

The Body Positivity Journal by Meghan Sylvester

The Gifts of Imperfection by Brené Brown

The Way of Integrity by Martha Beck

Women Who Run With the Wolves by Clarissa Pinkola Estés

Inspiration:

Amy Cuddy's TED Talk *"Your Body Language May Shape Who You Are"*

HeartMath Institute's research on how your heart literally emits electromagnetic fields that shift the energy around you: https://www.heartmath.org/research/research library/energetics/electricity-of-touch/

The Gateless Writing Methodology by Suzanne Kingsbury. For more information, visit gatelesswriting.com.

References

Brown, S. L., & Vaughan, C. C. (2009). *Play: How it shapes the brain, opens the imagination, and invigorates the soul.*

Carney, D. R., Cuddy, A. J. C., & Yap, A. J. (2010). *Power posing: Brief nonverbal displays affect neuroendocrine levels and risk tolerance. Psychological Science,* 21(10), 1363–1368.

Fowler, J. H., & Christakis, N. A. (2008). *Dynamic spread of happiness in a large social network: longitudinal analysis over 20 years in the Framingham Heart Study. BMJ,* 337, a2338.

Hatfield, E., Cacioppo, J. T., & Rapson, R. L. (1994). *Emotional Contagion.* Cambridge University Press.

Judith, A. (2004). *Wheels of life: A user's guide to the chakra system* (2ndZ ed.). Llewellyn Publications.

McCraty, R., Atkinson, M., & Tomasino, D. (2001). *Science of the Heart.* HeartMath Institute Research Center.

Neff, K. D., & Germer, C. K. (2013). *A pilot study and randomized controlled trial of the Mindful Self-Compassion program. Journal of Clinical Psychology,* 69(1), 28–44.

Panksepp, J. (2007). *Play and the regulation of affect. In Affective Neuroscience of the Child.*

Petrocchi, N., Ottaviani, C., & Couyoumdjian, A. (2017). *Compassion at the mirror: Exposure to a mirror increases the efficacy of a self-compassion manipulation in enhancing soothing positive affect and heart rate variability. The Journal of Positive Psychology,* 12(6), 525–536.

Porges, S. W. (2011). *The Polyvagal Theory: Neurophysiological Foundations of Emotions, Attachment, Communication, and Self-Regulation.* Norton.

Van der Kolk, B. (2014). *The Body Keeps the Score: Brain, Mind, and Body in the Healing of Trauma.* Penguin.

Acknowledgements

To my friends, thank you for cheering me on, celebrating every milestone, and reminding me who I am when I forget. Your belief in me has meant more than you know.

To Justin, my husband, my peacock, thank you for being my biggest champion. For watching the kids for endless hours so I could write in peace. For holding it down while I followed the thread of something sacred. This book wouldn't exist without your steady love.

To the women I've had the absolute pleasure of supporting—thank you. You trusted me to guide you, but the truth is you guided me, too. Your stories, your courage, your desire to come alive . . . it all shaped this book.

Lily, Ruby, and Happy, you are my constant reminders of what it means to be fully here. Thank you for your curiosity, your joy, and your ability to pull me into the present moment again and again. You've taught me how to live with wonder. I love being your mum!

To the women in my community, the dance teachers, the yoga instructors, the pilates guides, the health practitioners who helped me feel whole again, the creatives and leaders—I see you. Thank you for sharing your wild wisdom so generously. Moving with you, being led by you, returning to my body through your classes has been medicine. There is nothing more powerful than being guided by other women walking in their fullness.

Mum, thank you for being such a force. For modelling strength, resilience, and creative fire. So much of my voice was born from your example.

And to my dad in heaven, thank you for pulling strings for me, even from the other side. I feel your presence in the quiet miracles, the unexpected winks, the deep knowing that I'm never alone.

This book is the result of so many shared moments—sacred, simple, soulful. Thank you for being part of them.

About the Author

Meg Sylvester is a multi-passionate creative, speaker, author, and facilitator devoted to helping women wake up to their joy, creativity, and aliveness. Through soulful storytelling and playful, profound experiences, Meg guides others toward becoming their favourite selves—on their own terms. Her vibrant presence has inspired thousands around the world through transformative retreats, events, and digital content. She has collaborated with globally recognized brands, such as Free People, Proper Hotel, and Aviator Nation, and lit up stages at SXSW, Daybreaker, and Life is Beautiful Festival.

A trusted voice in the wellness space, Meg also partners with nonprofits and pioneers in mental health and education to uplift and empower communities. Meg lives in Boise, Idaho, with her husband of nearly two decades and their three wildly creative kids, who keep life beautifully full and deeply human.

Want to stay in the energy?

You can find Meg at www.megsylvester.com and on Instagram @meghansylvester, where she shares new ways to keep your spark alive through intentional girls trips, coaching, creativity, and joyful community. She'd love to stay connected.

First published in 2026 by Rock Point, an imprint of The Quarto Group,
135 West 36th Street, 13th Floor, New York, NY 10018, USA
(212) 779-4972   www.Quarto.com

EEA Representation, WTS Tax d.o.o.,
Žanova ulica 3, 4000 Kranj, Slovenia.
www.wts-tax.si

Rock Point titles are also available at discount for retail, wholesale, promotional, and bulk
purchase. For details, contact the Special Sales Manager by email at specialsales@quarto.com
or by mail at The Quarto Group, Attn: Special Sales Manager, 100 Cummings Center Suite 265D,
Beverly, MA 01915 USA.

10 9 8 7 6 5 4 3 2 1

ISBN: 979-8-3179-0107-3

Digital edition published in 2026
eISBN: 979-8-3179-0131-8

Group Publisher: Rage Kindelsperger
Editorial Director: Erin Canning
Creative Director: Laura Drew
Managing Editor: Cara Donaldson
Editor: Keyla Pizarro-Hernández
Cover and Interior Design: Raine Rath

Printed in Huizhou City, Guangdong, China TT122025

This book provides general information on various widely known and widely accepted images
that tend to evoke feelings of strength and confidence. However, it should not be relied upon
as recommending or promoting any specific diagnosis or method of treatment for a particular
condition, and it is not intended as a substitute for medical or mental health advice or for direct
diagnosis and treatment of a medical or mental health condition by a qualified physician.
Readers who have questions about a particular condition, possible treatments for that
condition, or possible reactions from the condition or its treatment should consult a physician
or other qualified health care professional.